☀ INSIGHT COMPACT GUIDE

JERSEY

Compact Guide: Jersey is the ultimate quick-reference guide to this, the largest of the Channel Islands. It tells you everything you need to know about the island's attractions, from miles of sandy beaches to prehistoric sites, from flora and fauna to forts and fortresses, from museums and manor houses to Gerald Durrell's zoo.

This is one of 133 Compact Guides produced by the editors of Insight Guides, whose books have set the standard for visual travel guides since 1970. Packed with information, arranged in easy-to-follow routes, and fully illustrated with photographs, this book not only steers you round Jersey but also gives you fascinating insights into local life.

D1147627

Star Attractions

An instant reference to some of Jersey's top attractions to help you set your priorities.

St Helier p14

Maritime Museum p15

Elizabeth Castle p20

Jersey War Tunnels p22

St Aubin p26

St Ouen's Bay p31

Lavender Farm p36

Gorey p45

Jersey Zoo p50

North Coast Path p52

Hamptonne Country Life Museum p35

Introduction

Places

Culture

Leisure

Practical Information

Jersey – Queen of the Channel

The French writer, Victor Hugo, who lived in exile in Jersey and Guernsey for 18 years, described the Channel Islands as *'Fragments of Europe dropped by France and picked up by England'*. Forming part of the Duchy of Normandy at the time of the Conquest in 1066, these dots in the shadow of France have been linked with the British Crown for more than 900 years. However, as self-governing islands and strongholds of ancient, semi-feudal laws, they are not truly British, nor are they French. English is now the accepted language, currency is pounds and pence, yet street and place names are French, the food has a French slant and the islands have a distinctly foreign flavour. Tourists are drawn by this combination of French flavour and British lifestyle – not to mention the location which is sufficiently far south to guarantee more daily hours of sun than anywhere else in Britain.

In recent years Jersey's holiday trade has declined through competition from cheap holidays to the hotter climes of southern Europe. To lure back visitors, the island is promoting itself as a year-round short-break destination, focusing on heritage, gastronomy, sport and action – as well as traditional beach holidays. With the advent of low-cost carriers (notably the twice daily flybmi service from Heathrow), the number of air passengers from the UK is on the rise again.

For a tiny island Jersey packs in plenty of attractions, from ancient castles and excellent museums to arts and crafts, sea sports and cycle tours, spas and adventure parks. But for most visitors it's the coastline which is the greatest allure. Jersey has 50 miles (80km) of shoreline and 20 miles (32km) of fine sandy beaches, swept clean by huge tides. Nowhere on the island lies more than 2½ miles (4km) from the sea. Moreover, the coastal scenery is extremely varied, from the towering cliffs of the north to the Atlantic rollers of the windswept west and the spacious unspoilt sands of the south.

Beachcombers

5

Bear at Durrell Wildlife

Location and size

The most southerly of the British Isles, Jersey lies in the Gulf of St Malo, 100 miles (160km) from the south coast of Britain, but just 14 miles (22km) from France. On most days Normandy is visible from the east coast of the island. The largest of the Channel Islands, Jersey is 9 miles (14km) east to west, 5 miles (8km) north to south and covers an area of 45 square miles (116 sq km). However, the 350 miles (560km) of roads, many of them narrow winding lanes, make the island feel much larger than it really is.

Jersey has two dependencies, both of them

St Brelade's Bay
Summer sun

Rule Britannia

offshore reefs: Les Minquiers, (commonly known as 'the Minkies'), 9 miles (14km) south of St Helier, and Les Ecréhous, 5 miles (8km) off the north-east coast. Neither is inhabited, but both have a customs depot and weekend huts. Ownership of the reefs has often been the subject of dispute between France and Britain, and the matter was taken to the International Court in the Hague in 1953. Although the court ruled in favour of Britain, there are still occasional attempts by French adventurers to take possession of the reefs.

The resident population of Jersey is 87,180, consisting of 52 percent Jersey, 35 percent British, 6 percent Portuguese and 7 percent other nationalities, including a large number of Polish residents.

Climate

Jersey has the highest average number of sunshine hours in the British Isles, although the summer temperatures are no higher than those in some parts of southern England. In the summer months the island has a daily average of eight hours of sunshine and an average maximum temperature of 68° F (20° C). As in the UK, there is always the risk of bad weather, but clouds are often quickly dispersed by the strong south-westerly winds. The best months to go are May to September, July and August being the hottest. The Atlantic sea temperatures are cool for swimming, averaging 62.8° F (17.1° C) in summer.

The island has one of the largest tidal movements in the world and the coastal landscape undergoes dramatic changes between high and low water. During spring tides Jersey's surface area increases from 45 to 63 square miles (72 to 100 sq km) and the vertical difference between high and low water can be as much as 40ft (12 metres).

Government

When William, Duke of Normandy, conquered England in 1066, the Channel Islands formed part of Normandy. When King John lost his Norman dominions to the French in 1204, the islanders had to choose either to stay with Normandy or remain loyal to the English crown. They chose the latter and were granted the right to retain their Norman laws and customs. Because the English monarch's authority over the islands stems historically from the role of Duke of Normandy, Jersey's royal toast is 'The Queen Our Duke'.

The island's constitutional relationship with the UK has been confirmed by successive royal charters, thus maintaining the independent judicial and parliamentary systems of the States of Jersey. Despite its loyalty to the British crown, Jersey is therefore not constitutionally part of the UK. Such is the island's independence that it even issues its own currency and it is effectively only in matters of foreign policy and defence that it is subordinate to the UK. The island is not part of the European Union, but when the UK joined in 1973, the Channel Islands managed to negotiate very favourable terms concerning the free movement of manufactured and agricultural goods.

Jersey's coat of arms

The constitution of the States of Jersey comprises the Lieutenant Governor, who is the Monarch's representative in the island, the Bailiff, the Dean of Jersey, the Attorney General and the Solicitor General – along with 12 senators, 12 parish constables and 29 deputies who are all democratically elected. Following the recommendation of a government review body to overhaul Jersey's ancient constitution, the old committee system was abolished and ministerial government introduced in 2005. A number of scrutiny panels (which hold public hearings) keep an eye on the policies of the executive.

The Bailiff heads the judiciary, with a chief magistrate and 12 honorary judges known as jurats. The island still retains the ancient institution of a non-paid, non-uniformed police force. Headed by the Constable, the members include Centeniers, Vingteniers and Constable Officers. This honorary police force, which works in conjunction with the paid, uniformed force, enjoys considerable authority and to this day maintains the exclusive right to charge suspects.

7

Maintaining standards

The legal system still retains certain feudal rights, one of which is the curious *Clameur de Haro* used, albeit rarely, to protect private property. With a witness either side the offended civilian goes down on bended knee and cries out: *'Haro! Haro! Haro! à l'aide, mon prince, on me fait tort'*. 'Haro' derives from 'Ahrou', the name given to Rollo the Viking, first Duke of Normandy and creator of the law. The rest translates: 'to my aid, my prince, I am being wronged'. The accused must then stop the offence until the case is heard in a court of law. If the Clameur is used without justification, the claimant is taken to court and fined.

Bouley Bay

Traditional costume at the Hamptonne Country Life Museum

Language

Until the 1960s French was still the official language of Jersey. Even today a few words of standard French are used by the court and legal professions. Prayers are said in French before States and court sittings and the parliament votes *pour* or *contre*. Not so long ago a Jerseyman would have spoken English, French and the ancient Jersey-Norman *patois* known as Jèrriais.

Jèrriais had virtually died out but enjoyed a revival during the German Occupation as a useful means of covert communication, and today it can very occasionally be heard used by elderly Jersiais (the people who speak it) at rural events such as the cattle or agricultural auctions. Jersey-French language groups are anxious to keep this historic language alive and the signs at the airport and harbour now wish visitors *'beinv'nue a Jèrri'*.

The English language was first introduced to Jersey in the 18th century, and is now spoken by all the islanders. Street names on the island still carry their French names, often very different from the English names they were later given, e.g. La Rue de Derrière (King Street), La Rue des Trois Pigeons (Hill Street) and La Rue Trousse Cotillon (Church Street, but in French 'Pick up your Petticoat Street'). Most of the place names on the island retain their French names, and pronounciation still gives rise to some confusion for English visitors. Ouaisné, for example, is pronounced *Waynay*, and St Ouen, *Saint Wan*.

Economy and environment

Finance today is the main pillar of the economy. The financial services industry employs over 25 percent of the working population. Since Napoleonic times Jersey has attracted high-earning immigrants seeking to benefit from the island's desirable way of life and advantageous tax laws. Among the UK celebrities who have set up home here are TV personality Alan Wicker, musician Gilbert O'Sullivan, golfer Ian Woosnam and best-selling author Jack Higgins. Today's high earners are actively encouraged through the High Value Residency initiative whereby applications are assessed for suitability on social and economic grounds, including paying taxes in excess of £100,000 per annum.

The local breed

Agriculture was formerly the mainstay of the economy. The Jersey cow, symbol of the island, is famous for its rich, golden high-fat milk, and the 'Jersey Royal', exported to the UK, is unmatched among new potatoes. However, agriculture and horticulture have suffered as a result of fierce competition from mainland Europe.

The tourism industry has seen a decade of decline reversed thanks to the low-cost airlines. To meet changing demands, a £100 million investment in tourism has financed the regeneration of old-fashioned hotels, equipping them with sleek spas and wi-fi connections. At the other end of the scale, visitors can stay in simple but stunningly located forts, follies and towers which have been converted by Jersey Heritage Trust to provide short breaks with a difference.

The island's beaches are far less crowded than those at popular European resorts and the sands are washed by some of the cleanest waters in Europe, aided by an award-winning ultra-violet sewage treatment system. Green lanes, reducing the speed limit on some country lanes to 15 mph, have encouraged cyclists and pedestrians, and clearly marked cycle routes now cover 96 miles (155km) of coast and countryside. On the negative side, Jersey still has a major traffic problem, especially in St Helier; it also generates a phenomenal amount of rubbish and the spread of reclamation site wastelands is evidence that the island is not yet entirely committed to restraint and recycling.

Flora and fauna

Jersey's mild oceanic climate and varied habitats attract flora and fauna which are rare or non-existent in mainland Britain. Among these are the loose-flowered orchid, or Jersey orchid, the agile frog, the Jersey green lizard and the Glanville fritillary butterfly. The rarest of the birds is the tiny and elusive Dartford warbler, which inhabits the gorse-strewn heathlands.

The Jersey green lizard

Les Mieilles Conservation Area, stretching almost the full length of Jersey's west coast, is a haven for naturalists. Sand dunes, scrub, freshwater ponds, reed beds and the adjacent seashore provide a variety of habitats for plants, birds and marine life. Les Blanches Banques to the south is regarded as the fourth most important sand dune system in Europe, supporting countless species of plants. Of these, 17 are recorded in the British Red Data Book of endangered and vulnerable plants.

Jersey lilies

The reed beds and marshy surrounds of St Ouen's Pond to the north lure scores of migratory birds, including sedge warblers and bearded reedlings. This was the first nesting site in the British Isles for Cetti's warbler and the nest can be seen in the Jersey Museum in St Helier.

Other prime areas for ornithologists are the low-lying south and southeast coast, where the vast expanse of mud, sand and rocky outcrops exposed at low tide provides a rich breeding ground for thousands of wintering waders, gulls and wildfowl. Plovers, redshank, turnstone, dunlin, bar-tailed godwits, curlew and oystercatchers can be seen on an incoming tide along the rocky shore.

Along the north coast, shags breed on the steep cliffs, sharing their rocky ledges with fulmars; and a small colony of puffins returns each year to its cliff-side burrows on the northwest coast. Early morning and evening are the best time to see the birds.

Wild ducks

Historical Highlights

c6,500BC Previously attached to the land mass of Europe, Jersey becomes an island.

4,850–2,850BC The Neolithic Period. Settlers plant crops, raise animals, create flint tools, stone axes, pottery and querns (hand-mills for grinding cereals). Megalithic tombs or dolmens are erected, of which La Hougue Bie *(see page 44)* is the finest example. Archaeological discoveries include teeth of Neanderthal man, flint tools and bones of woolly mammoths and rhinos at La Cotte de St Brelade.

2,250–600BC Bronze Age. Bronze is used for weapons, jewellery and other luxury items. Late Bronze Age finds include the spectacular gold torque, found in St Helier. This long ornament of twisted gold was probably wrapped around parts of the body as decoration.

600BC–AD350 Iron Age. Larger settlements develop on the island. The main archaeological finds are hoards of coins from the 1st century BC. These may have been buried as news came of Romans sweeping northwestwards through France.

56BC Channel Islands become part of Gaul, but there is little evidence of the Roman Occupation.

6th and 7th centuries AD Britons, fleeing from the Saxons, arrive in Jersey via Brittany and bring Christianity to the island. St Helier arrives in Jersey in the 6th century and founds a hermitage in a cave near what is now Elizabeth Castle. Martyred by pirates in 555, he becomes the patron saint of the island.

9th century Vikings arrive in their longboats and ravage the islands.

933 King Rollo's son, William Longsword, annexes the Cotentin peninsula and the Channel Islands to the Duchy of Normandy. Normans make their mark with their code of laws, the foundation of the Common Law of the Channel Islands, their language (Norman-French) and seafaring traditions. Feudalism is introduced.

1066 Battle of Hastings. William the Conqueror gains the English crown and the Channel Islands become part of the Anglo-Norman realm.

1204 King John loses Normandy to King Philip of France. Channel Islands remain loyal to the English sovereign.

1215 In return for their allegiance, King John grants the Channel Islands customs and privileges, tantamount to self-government, which have since been confirmed by every English monarch. France is now the enemy and for the next 650 years the island is frequently threatened by French raids.

1200–1450 Construction of Mont Orgueil (Gorey Castle) to defend Gorey and Grouville Bays against French attacks. The castle is the main fortress on the island until the construction of Elizabeth Castle in the late 16th century. In 1338 Bertrand du Guesclin, Constable of France, invades the island but Mont Orgueil withstands the siege.

1461–8 Mont Orgueil captured by the French during the Wars of the Roses. Jersey under French rule for seven years, until it is retaken by Edward IV of England.

1483 Agreement between Edward IV and Louis XI of France that the Channel Islands and surrounding waters should be regarded as neutral in the event of war. (Agreement abolished in 1689.)

1547 The Reformation comes to Jersey, resulting in the destruction of all church stained glass, statuary, fonts, small chapels and roadside crosses. In 1550 all church property is sold by the Royal Commissioners. French Protestants (Huguenots) flee from Normandy to Jersey. When Elizabeth I comes to the throne, Jersey adopts Calvinism.

1500–1600 Construction of Elizabeth Castle on the islet of St Helier. Sir Walter Raleigh, Governor of Jersey from 1600 to 1604, names it after Queen Elizabeth I.

1608 States Act passed prohibiting the lucrative knitting of socks by men, women and children during the harvest period to encourage more people to work on the land.

1642–47 In the English Civil War, Jersey supports the Royalists.

1649 Charles I is beheaded. Charles II, then Prince of Wales, who takes refuge in Jersey, is proclaimed king by Sir George Carteret, Governor of the island. He later takes refuge again in Jersey as exiled King of England. As a reward, he gives Smith's Island and some neighbouring islets off Virginia to Sir George Carteret with permission to settle. These are renamed New Jersey.

1651 Following Cromwell's defeat of the Royalists, Parliamentarians are sent from England to Jersey to put down the Royalist resistance. St Aubin's Fort and Mont Orgueil are taken, but Elizabeth Castle withstands a siege of seven weeks. Carteret surrenders after an enemy bomb blows up the arsenal.

Late 17th century Commerce thrives, merchant sailors and shipbuilders grow rich on codfishing in Newfoundland. Fine merchants' houses built in St Aubin.

1779–1835 Construction of 30 coastal towers for defence of the island from the French.

1781 Battle of Jersey. French attempt to take over the island, under the command of Baron de Rullecourt. The heroic Major Peirson leads the local militia to victory in the Battle of Jersey, which takes place in St Helier's Royal Square. Both Peirson and De Rullecourt are killed in action.

1787 John Wesley visits Jersey, inspiring the Methodist movement.

1789 French Revolution brings aristocratic refugees, fleeing from the Reign of Terror.

1806–14 In anticipation of an attack by France, construction starts on Fort Regent, St Helier.

1815 After the French defeat at Waterloo, attacks from the French cease and Fort Regent is never used to defend St Helier. Influx of British army officers to Jersey, retired on half-pension.

1830s Heyday of the oyster industry.

1846 Queen Victoria visits Jersey. Victoria College opened in 1852 as a memorial to her visit.

1870 The Jersey railway is opened. St Helier is linked to Grouville in 1873 and to St Aubin in 1884, extending to Corbière in 1899.

1880s Steam ships mark the start of the decline of Jersey's lucrative shipbuilding trade.

1936 The Jersey Railway forced to close because of competition from buses and a fire which destroys most of the rolling stock at St Aubin.

1937 Airport opens at St Peter.

1940 Channel Islands demilitarised. 10,000 evacuated from Jersey. On 28 June the Germans bomb St Helier and demand peaceful surrender on 1 July. German forces move into Jersey.

1940–44 The German Occupation. The island is heavily fortified, and foreign prisoners are brought to the island to build defences. Rationing is introduced and supplies of food, fuel and medicine decline, particularly after D-Day.

1945 In the last months of the Occupation the neutral Swedish vessel, the *SS Vega*, brings Red Cross food parcels and other essential provisions.

9 May 1945 Liberation of the Channel Islands by British forces. King George VI and Queen Elizabeth visit the islands the following month.

1946 Royal Jersey Militia is disbanded after 600 years of service.

1948 English and French become the two official languages of the Jersey. In practice, government business is conducted in English only.

1973 Britain joins the European Community. Special terms are agreed for the Channel Islands.

1980s Offshore finance becomes the main source of States revenue.

2004 Jersey celebrates 800 years of allegiance to the Crown.

2005 The Queen visits Jersey to mark the 60th anniversary of the liberation of the Channel Islands. The States of Jersey adopt modern ministerial government, replacing the antiquated committee system.

2005–2007 Over £100 million is pumped into the States' tourist industry. Revamping of old hotels and the opening in November 2007 of the 190-room Radisson SAS hotel on the new Waterfront.

Excursions from St Helier

Jersey War Tunnels

Les Charrières Malorey, St Lawrence *See map, pages 24–5*

The Channel Islands were the only British territories to be invaded by German forces in World War II. Tiny possessions they may have been, but Hitler saw them as the first step to his intended invasion of the United Kingdom. With remarkable speed, the islands were turned into impregnable fortresses. Thousands of forced, foreign labourers were used in the construction of defences around Jersey and today the bunkers, towers and gun emplacements stand out as stark reminders of those harrowing five years.

The most remarkable engineering feat of the Occupation is the ★★★ **Jersey War Tunnels** (Feb–Dec, 10am–6pm, last admission 4.30pm; www.jerseywartunnels.com). From St Helier follow the signs to the west, and keep on the A1 by branching right at the end of the Esplanade. Keep on this inner road as far as Bel Royal, turn right on to the A11 and follow the signs for the War Tunnels.

The massive network of tunnels and galleries, hewn from solid rock with gunpowder and handtools, was the work of thousands of forced labourers and Russian prisoners-of-war who toiled here in harsh conditions. Creating the tunnels entailed the removal of 43,900 tonnes of rock and the cladding of 6,000 cubic metres of concrete.

The underground centre was originally designed as a bomb-proof artillery barracks, to protect the entire garrison of around 12,000 men against assault from sea or air. Sixteen tunnels were planned for the use of ammunition storage, armoured vehicles, fuel and food. However, the complex was never completed, for in the weeks leading to D-Day, with an Allied invasion looming, orders were given for the

5pm). Lying offshore from the Waterfront Centre *(see map, page 24–5)*, this can be reached by the causeway leading to the islet in St Aubin's Bay where the castle stands. The causeway (about ¾ mile/1km long) can be crossed on foot at low water, or by amphibious ferry (not included in the castle entrance fee) which departs from the West Park slipway and travels at all tides.

Construction on the castle began in the late 16th century, by which time Mont Orgueil, built for bows and arrows *(see page 45)*, was becoming increasingly vulnerable. Sir Walter Raleigh, the island's governor, who lived at the castle from 1600, called it Fort Isabella Bellissima (Elizabeth the most Beautiful), in tribute to his Queen, Elizabeth I.

It was not until the 1640s when Jersey had been drawn into the English Civil War that the castle, which by now had grown considerably in size, came into its own. Charles II, then Prince of Wales, took refuge here, and did so again after the execution of his father, when Jersey proclaimed him King Charles II. During the war, Sir Philip Carteret, then Governor, sustained a siege here for 50 days and the castle was the last of Jersey's strongholds to surrender. Defeat came in December 1651 when a shell from from St Helier Hill (now Fort Regent) hit the abbey church and exploded the powder magazine.

The gun is fired at noon

21

The fortifications you see today date mainly from the 17th century, with the Guard House, hospital and workshops added in the early 19th century. The buildings around the Parade Ground house an exhibition covering the history of the castle, the museum café and the **Royal Jersey Militia Museum**, which has an exhibition of uniforms, medals and other military memorabilia. The Jersey Militia served the island for around 600 years and in their heyday numbered over 6,000 local men, divided into five regiments. To reinforce the military theme, Gunner Graves fires the noonday gun, and male visitors may be dragooned into marching the Parade Ground.

Hermitage Rock

The path behind the Militia Museum affords views over the breakwater to **Hermitage Rock**, home of the hermit who gave his name to the capital and parish. Son of a Belgian noble, he came to Jersey in the 6th century to devote his life to prayer, but was hacked to death by Saxon pirates in AD555. Legend has it that he picked up his head and carried on walking, much to the horror of the pirates. In the 12th century a small oratory was built over his cave and every year on the Sunday closest to 16 July a pilgrimage makes its way here, and a wreath is laid in his memory. For the best views of the coast, climb up to the gunnery control tower built by the Germans who modernised the castle with guns, bunkers and battlements.

The Waterfront Centre

Take the Puddle Duck (above) to Elizabeth Castle (below)

interactive videos and touch screens. Exhibits cover all aspects of the island including interesting sections on traditions and trades specific to Jersey, such as oyster catching, shipbuilding and knitting. The exhibition starts with a recreation of the Old Stone Age site of La Cotte de St Brelade *(see Culture, page 59)*, showing the figures of Paleolithic man on the rockface and the bones of pre-historic woolly rhino found at the foot of the cave. Jersey was then part of the Continent and a display (on the first floor) shows how the sea level rose and the Channel Islands were formed.

The second floor is devoted to works by Jersey artists, including 19th-century seascapes and landscapes and John Everett Millais' portrait of Jersey's most famous daughter Lillie Langtry. The top floor rooms, comprising school room and bedrooms, have been carefully reconstructed to show how they would have looked in Victorian times when the house was occupied by a doctor and his family.

For many visitors the favourite museum display is the Lillie Langtry memorabilia. Born Emilie Charlotte Le Breton in 1853, the daughter of a philandering Jersey dean, she married a wealthy widower in 1874. Two years later she took London society by storm with her beauty and charm. 'The Jersey Lily' became the mistress of the Prince of Wales, subsequently Edward VII, and later caused a further sensation by becoming the first society woman to take to the stage. The 'second Helen of Troy', as Oscar Wilde called her, died in Jersey in 1929 and is buried in the graveyard of St Saviour's Church.

Exit the museum by the front entrance and look back at the facade. This handsome Georgian house, which once stood on the waterfront, belonged to a wealthy shipowner who contributed in 1820 to the cost of land reclamation and a harbour building scheme (now Commercial Buildings).

St Helier's shore on the west side is home to the huge new **Waterfront Centre** comprising housing developments, a leisure centre, multiplex cinema, night club, bars and fast food outlets. The multi-storey, international Radisson SAS hotel right on the waterfront opened in November 2007.

Intended as 'the new maritime quarter', reconnecting the town with the seashore, the waterfront development continually comes under fire for its utilitarian and stark architectural style. It will be several years before completion and there is currently heated debate as to how the shore should be connected to the centre. Meanwhile, most tourists (and many islanders) are giving it a wide berth.

No visit to St Helier is really complete without seeing ★★★ **Elizabeth Castle**, one of Jersey's major historic monuments (Easter–Oct daily 10am–6pm, last admission century Thesaurus Bookshop – antiquarian and out-of-print specialists.

At the next crossroads look to your right for the classical facade of the **Wesley Grove Methodist Church** (1847) at the top end of Halkett Place. John Wesley, who visited Jersey, Guernsey and Alderney, had a profound influence on the islanders and, by the 1820s, chapels, large and small, in the vernacular, Gothic or classical style were appearing all over the islands. This one used to seat 1,600. Methodism still has a strong influence on many of the islanders and several of the churches are still in use.

The prominent building with the pink, blue and russet stuccowork which you pass going up to the church, on the other side of the road, is the late Victorian Mechanics Institute. Originally called the Albert Hall, it's now a snooker club. Beyond it, the public library was opened by the Queen in 1989.

Make your way back along Halkett Place, to the far end of the street, passing en route the Evangelical Church, the market, and just before the end of the street on your right, the public entrance to the States Chamber, where the Order Paper for the day is normally posted. At the top, Hill Street, bristling with brass nameplates, is the street of advocates. Turn right into Mulcaster Street, then left for Pier Road. Just up the hill on the right is **La Société Jersiaise**, founded in 1873 for study and research into all matters relating to Jersey. The society runs an excellent library (Sat 10am–4.30pm) and maintains the neighbouring ★★★ **Jersey Museum ❾** (daily 9.30am–5pm). This can be reached by taking the steps down to the courtyard and following the signs.

The museum, which has won major national awards, tells the story of Jersey from prehistoric to present times. Displays are highly informative and often enlivened by

The award-winning Jersey Museum with dairy exhibits

19

Satyr at the Jersey Museum

The Peirson

Central Market display

Anthony Trollope's letterbox

message that the Channel Islands were to be liberated. To the east of the Royal Court is the States Chamber, whose Public Gallery, accessed on the far side from Halkett Place, is open to visitors every other Tuesday when the States are in session. In the centre of the square a stone commemorates the dramatic Battle of Jersey that took place here in 1781. Baron de Rullecourt arrived secretly at La Rocque in the southeast corner of the island and led his small army to St Helier, before the islanders awoke. The Lieutenant-Governor, still in bed, was tricked into believing that De Rullecourt had a much larger army, and surrendered. But a gallant young officer, Major Francis Peirson, ignored the surrender, rallied the troops, and after a brief but bloody battle, defeated the French in Royal Square. Both De Rullecourt and Peirson were mortally wounded and shot marks can still be seen on the building in the corner of the square which is now the Peirson pub. This was the last attempt by France to capture the island. Jersey's young hero was immortalized in John Singleton Copley's painting of *The Death of Major Peirson* at London's Tate Britain Gallery, a copy of which hangs in the Royal Court.

Peirson Place beside the pub leads to **King Street**, a busy pedestrianised shopping thoroughfare. Opposite you, Woolworths was formerly the grounds of the Governor's House. Turn right along King Street for Halkett Place, named after a former Lt Governor of Jersey who served with distinction at the Battle of Waterloo.

Cross the street and turn left to get to the ★★ **Central Market** ❼ (Mon–Sat 7.30am–5.30pm, except Thur 7.30am–1pm). This is a fine Victorian building with cast iron columns supporting the glass roof and an ornate circular fountain with cherubs, foliage and live goldfish. Market stalls were banned from Royal Square in 1800 and the new site chosen on the corner of Halkett Place and Beresford Street. The market erected here was pulled down and replaced by a new one in 1882. A favourite venue for both locals and tourists, Central Market has 40 stalls selling fresh produce, flowers, Jersey lily bulbs, meat, cheese, bread and groceries. Outside the post office the hexagonal letterbox (1851) designed by the novelist Anthony Trollope, was one of the very first in the British Isles.

Leave the market at the Beresford Street exit and turn right. Across the road, the ★ **Fish Market** ❽ has a fine selection of conger eel, bass, wrasse, grey mullet, shrimps, live lobsters, spider and chancre crabs and many other locally caught species. Head down here at 7.30am to see the catch of the day arrive or make it later in the day for a seafood snack and glass of wine at the Atlantique Seafood Bar. At the far exit, turn left along Minden Place, cross Castle Street, and note on the right the 19th-

Locals sought refuge here in times of crisis, elections were held here, bells were rung when enemy ships were sighted and orders were issued by the Constable. Major Peirson, hero of the Battle of Jersey *(see page 18)* is buried in the church, while Baron de Rullecourt, who led the enemy, has a small stone memorial in the graveyard.

Leave the church by the north side for Church Street. The name of the street looks somewhat prosaic beside the former French name of La Rue Trousse Cotillon or Pick Up Your Petticoat Street. This dates from a less salubrious era when ladies had to lift up their dresses to avoid the drains and sewers. Turning left into the street, note the house on the opposite side of the road (now the United Club), where John Wesley preached his gospel of Methodism in 1787. Further along on the corner is Jersey's first library, a Georgian building and one of the first on the island to be made of brick.

At the end of Library Place, to the left, the obelisk was erected in 1855 in recognition of Pierre le Sueur, who was responsible for the underground sewage system.

Royal Square and insignia

From Church Street turn into ★★★ **Royal Square ❺**, formerly the marketplace, where proclamations were made, public executions took place, the occasional witch was burnt and criminals awaited trial in an iron cage. Today it is a peaceful square, shaded by horse-chestnut trees. The back of the United Club is the Registry Office, now used by UK couples taking advantage of a law which now enables them to get married in Jersey. The building was formerly the corn market and inside original granite arches have been preserved. The 'V' for Victory which you can see marked in the paving in front of the building was secretly cut by a local stonemason who was re-laying the flagstones during the Occupation. Discovery of the act may well have led to deportation so he hid the 'V' under a layer of sand. The letters 'EGA' and '1945' were later added to commemorate the Swedish Red Cross vessel, *SS Vega*, which arrived towards the end of the Occupation with 750 tons of food parcels, relieving both occupiers and islanders from near-starvation.

The ostentatious **gilded statue** in the square depicts King George II (1727–60), dressed as Caesar, but wearing the Order of the Garter around his thigh. It was placed here and the square renamed when the King donated £200 towards the creation of St Helier's first harbour.

On the south side of Royal Square, the central building is the **Royal Court** (1866) ❻, the island's court of justice, with the arms of George II above the entrance. It was from the balcony to the right that Alexander Coutanche, Bailiff of Jersey, hoisted the Union Jack on 8 May 1945 and relayed to the huge crowds Churchill's

Church of St Helier

up Mulcaster Street, the Lamplighter pub is decorated with stuccowork depicting the figure of Britannia between two cherubs and a garland of fruit below. This was the work of Turnkey Giffard, a prison warden who entertained his inmates by showing them how to carve. Take the next turning left into Bond Street, where Regency and Victorian buildings retain some of their original features. On the right the ★ **Church of St Helier** ❹ is named after the 6th-century hermit who preached from a rock beside what is now Elizabeth Castle *(see page 20)*. The gate at the far end of the railings formed part of a screen used to segregate male and female prisoners during services in the Debtors' Prison. The church was formerly the hub of town life.

ST HELIER

of the German navy during the Occupation. The square used to be the terminus of the Jersey Railway which served the south and east coasts, and it was from the rear of this building that some 2,200 residents were deported to Germany in September 1942.

Up on Mont de la Ville, overlooking the town, the walls and bastions below the modern white dome survive from the original **Fort Regent**, built at enormous expense in 1806–14 against the threat of French invasion. Troops were stationed here for many years, but it was never actually used to defend the island. In 1958 the fort was sold back to the States for £14,500, the original price of the land, and the building was then converted into a huge leisure centre, complete with sports facilities, concert hall, exhibitions and entertainment. The mast, to the far left, is the last working signal station in the British Isles. Dating from 1708, it is now used to signal weather warnings, high tides, shipping movements and anniversaries. The latest addition is the orange pennant which goes up when the plane carrying the daily national newspapers has left London and is lowered to half mast when it lands. The Union Jack on the west bastion is lowered to half mast only when a monarch dies, though an exception was made on the death of Diana, Princess of Wales.

Across the busy A1 south of Liberation Square, and looking like something out of Disneyland, the world's largest **Steam Clock** is modelled on a 19th-century paddle steamer. Wait long enough and it will start to foam, whistle and chime. Also on the waterfront stands the ★★★ **Maritime Museum** ❷ (daily 9.30am–5pm), housed in a restored warehouse on North Quay. The museum explores every aspect of the island's links with the sea, bringing to life its former role as a seafaring state. The museum offers plenty of hands-on exhibits and other activities. Visitors can feel the pull of the currents and the power of the sea, build a boat and sail it in the wave tank, listen to legends of the sea and watch the routes around the world made by Jersey vessels.

Within the same building and covered in the admission charge is the ★★ **Occupation Tapestry Gallery** ❸. This excellent display comprises 12 separate tapestries depicting scenes from the Occupation. These historically accurate and carefully worked scenes were created by the 12 Jersey parishes. The themes range from the Outbreak of War and Deportation to the Daily Life of Civilians, such as the school-room scene of a boy yawning in a German lesson.

Return to Liberation Square and, on the far side, cross the Esplanade. Take the road leading up from the Southampton Hotel and cross over Wharf Street. Half way

15

The Steam Clock

Boat building at the Maritime Museum

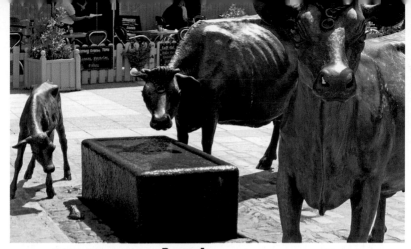

Cow sculpture, West's Centre

Preceding pages: Bonne Nuit Bay

Liberation Sculpture

Route 1

St Helier

Liberation Square – Maritime Museum – Occupation Tapestry – Church of St Helier – Royal Square – Central Market and Fish Market – Jersey Museum – Elizabeth Castle *See map on page 16*

St Helier, the capital of Jersey and its only real town, is the seat of the island's government and administration. It is not a place of great elegance and most of the older buildings have been demolished; however, it is home to the two best museums on the island, an historic castle and a central square steeped in history. Although many of the streets are thronged with traffic, the main shopping throughfares, with large stores, boutiques and lively food markets, are pedestrianised. The walk takes you through the historic centre, then out of the centre along the Esplanade to Elizabeth Castle.

Start at **Liberation Square ❶**, which was opened by Prince Charles on 9 May 1995, the 50th anniversary of the Liberation of the island from German Occupation. It was here that huge crowds gathered to see the British fleet sailing in to release the islanders after five long years under German rule. The prominent ★ **Liberation Sculpture** enlivens an otherwise unremarkable square, surrounded by a hotchpotch of architecture. The bronze group of figures, clutching at the Union Jack represent, from left to right: a Jersey couple of sufficient years to have witnessed the Occupation, a liberator, a Jersey fisherman and a farmer with his wife and children. Overlooking the square on the north side the Pomme d'Or Hotel was the headquarters

complex to be turned into a casualty receiving station. Five wards were each designed to cope with 100 casualties. Unfinished tunnels were sealed off and the site was equipped with operating theatre, recovery room, hospital wards, doctors' and nurses' quarters, Officers' Mess, escape shaft, central heating, air conditioning and telephone exchange.

Officers' Mess

The anticipated invasion never took place and the occupying forces surrendered peacefully on 9 May 1945. The hospital wards have been preserved or reconstructed, and the dark dripping tunnels have been maintained in their original, unfinished state. Inside the tunnels is the Captive Island exhibition, a poignant interpretation of life under the Nazi yoke, taking visitors from 'Threatened Island', through to 'Daily Life', 'Resistance' and ultimately 'Liberation'. Instead of a ticket, visitors are given an identity card relating to an individual who features in the exhibition. Many of these, including deportees, housewives and forced labourers, relate their experiences through video and sound installations. The exhibits include a chillingly accurate reconstruction of the operating theatre, ready for the first casualty from an Allied invasion that never happened. This comprehensive museum also features an exhibition dedicated to Violette Szabo, a young secret agent who was caught and executed at Ravensbrück concentration camp; and the Garden of Reflection, which records details of those who died as a direct consequence of the occupation.

The Living Legend *See map, pages 24–5*

The **Living Legend** (Apr–Oct, daily 10am–5pm; Mar–Nov, Sat–Wed only 10am–5pm) is an extensive purpose-built village offering a host of activities. From St Helier take the A1 going westwards as far as Bel Royal, turn right on to the A11, then follow the signs.

Within the 9-acre (4-hectare) site is a craft and shopping village, landscaped gardens, street entertainment, formula-one style karting track, children's playground and two 18-hole adventure golf courses whose multi-level holes among caves, lakes and waterfalls present an amusing diversion for all ages. But what makes a visit here really worthwhile is the ★ **Jersey Experience** – a multi-sensory recreation of the history and traditions of the island. With its dramatic special effects and lively dialogue, this is a firm favourite with children. Visitors start on the deck of a Victorian paddle steamer destined for St Helier, then, from a deck devoted to the island's millionaires, descend down the dark winding tunnel of time, encountering characters and creatures from local legends. Further down at 'the Island in the Sea', secrets are revealed of smugglers, shipwrecks and maritime myths. The auditorium is a mock-up of the Manoir de la Brequette, a manor house lost beneath the sea centuries ago. This is where the story of the island begins.

Jersey Experience: recreating the past

ROUTES 2, 3 & 4

| 0 | | 2 km |
| 0 | | 2 miles |

Ronez Point

St John's Bay

Fremont Point

Belle Hougue Point

La Colombière

Bonne Nuit Bay

Wolf's Caves

St John

Vicard Point

133

Les Platons

Leicester Battery

Bouley Bay

L'Etacquerel

Continued from page 38

St John's Village

La Hougue Boëte

A10

A9

Hautes Croix

A8

Bouley Bay

Jardin d'Olivet

Lion Park/ Jersey Gold

Handois Reservoir

A9

Trinity Village

Les Augrès Manor

Carrefour Selous

x Rues

Hamptonne Country Life Museum

Trinity

Durrell Wildlife

St Martin

Continued on page 38

St Lawrence

Pallot Heritage Steam Museum

St Lawrence's Church

Dannemarche Reservoir

Becquet Vincent

Victoria Village

Waterworks Valley

A8

Augrès

Eric Young Orchid Foundation

Grands-Vaux Reservoir

Maufant

Jersey War Tunnels

Millbrook Reservoir

St Helier

A8

3

St Saviour

La Hougue Bie

Five Oaks

La Hougue Bie

A11

A10

Bel Royal

A7

A2

Millbrook

A1

St Matthew's

First Tower

3

2

A9

A8

St Saviour's Church

A6

4

St Aubin's Bay

A1

ST HELIER

A7

Grouville

1

Grouville Arsenal

The Waterfront Centre

A3

Elizabeth Castle

A4

Dicq

A5

Samarès Manor

Mont Ubé

Nicolle Tower

St Clements

Grève d'Azette Bay

St Clement

La Haguais

Torquay, Portsmouth, Poole, Weymouth, Guernsey, Alderney, Sark

St Malo, Granville

Green Island

St Clement's Bay

Route 2

Surf and Sand

St Aubin – Portelet Bay – St Brelade's Bay – Beauport – Corbière Lighthouse – St Ouen's Bay and Village
See map, pages 24–5

Occupation reminder at St Ouen's

The route takes in the best of Jersey's beaches, from the sheltered, sandy bays of the south to the dramatic west coast where surfers ride the big Atlantic swell. For most of the way the route follows the coast, revealing spectacular cliffs, quiet coves and, in the southwest corner of the island, the treacherous rocks around Corbière lighthouse, landmark of the island.

Leave St Helier via the Esplanade, following the signs for 'The West' and St Aubin, keeping to the coast all the way. The gently curving, south-facing St Aubin's Bay stretches for three miles between St Helier and the town of St Aubin. At the near end, Elizabeth Castle *(see Route 1, page 20)* stands on the rocks offshore. The seafront promenade, which used to be the Western Railway Line, stretches the length of the beach. During spring tides, giant waves crash over the wall here and sand bags can often be seen protecting the small streets leading up from the coastal road. At Bel Royal, where the A1 and A2 converge, keep to the coast road for St Aubin's Harbour.

★★ **St Aubin** is a smaller, prettier place than St Helier, and lends itself to seaside strolls and leisurely lunches at inviting al fresco restaurants. Named after the Bishop of Angers, protector against pirates, the town ironically acquired much of its wealth through profiteering and in the 17th and 18th centuries it was the main port on the

St Aubin

island. During the English Civil War many a British vessel was captured and plundered by Sir George Carteret, the Royalist governor of the island. Such were the losses of British ships that parliamentary forces were sent by Cromwell to put down the Royalist resistance. Fortunes were also made by the more honourable trades of ship-building and codfishing in Newfoundland. Rich merchants built themselves fine four-storey houses, often equipped with huge cellars to store the booty. Some of the bulwarks stood on the seashore prior to the construction of the harbour and had spectacular roof outlooks for viewing the return of the fleet. One of the finest still standing is the **Old Court House**, overlooking the harbour, and now a hotel and restaurant. The loot was stored in the cellars and then divided in what was then the Court Room, presided over by the judges. The building had its moment of fame as the pub which featured strongly in *Bergerac,* the popular BBC Television cops and robbers series of the 1980s and early 90s.

Al fresco at the Old Court House

At the end of the quayside stands the **Royal Channel Islands Yacht Club**, whose first female member was Lillie Langtry *(see page 20)*. The strategically located **St Aubin's Fort** was built to command the western end of the bay in the mid-16th century. Persistent threats of invasion led to additional fortifications over the centuries, the most recent of which were built by the Germans during the Occupation. You can explore the fort by walking across the wet sands at low tide.

27

Yacht Club insignia

Parallel to the coast road, the high street, known also as Rue du Crocquet, used to be the main thoroughfare (for horses and carts) linking St Aubin with St Helier. The houses, many in local granite, were built by wealthy merchants at the end of the 17th century. The ones on your right would have backed directly on to the sea, enabling vessels to load and unload. Keep going to the top of the road for fine views across the bay.

Shell Garden

Turn inland from St Aubin along the A13, which climbs up the wooded valley towards St Brelade. On this steep road you are unlikely to miss the **Shell Garden** (Apr–Oct 9.45am–4.45pm), decorated with thousands of seashells. The owner has been adding to his collection since 1957. After ½ mile (1km) turn left at the corner shop along the Route de Noirmont and when you come to the small cross-roads, take the left turn just beyond it for ★ **Noirmont Point**. This windswept headland, once known as Niger Mons or Black Hill, after the dark clouds which gather here, was acquired by the States of Jersey to commemorate the islanders who died in World War II. A prominent relic of the Occupation is the huge underground Command Bunker of the former German coast artillery battery,

Portelet Bay

complete with a large observation tower brooding on the clifftop. The bunker has been carefully restored by the Channel Islands German Occupation Society and is open to the public on Thursday evenings (7–9pm) and some Monday mornings (10am–noon). The Coastal Artillery gun to the left of it originally stood at La Coupe, on the northeast coast, but after the war it was thrown over the cliffs by the British, then recovered in 1979.

Return to the junction and turn left for ★★ **Portelet Bay**. Park the car at the top of the cliff, by the Portelet Inn, admire the views from the top of the cliff and/or walk down the long flight of steps to the delightful sheltered bay below. The little island, accessible at low tide, is properly called the Ile au Guerdain but more popularly known as Janvrin's Tomb, after the sea captain who was buried here. When Janvrin was returning with his ship from plague-infested Nantes in France in 1721, he was refused entry to St Aubin's harbour for fear of contamination. Janvrin fell victim himself and, since his body was not allowed ashore, he was given a burial on the island. The body was later transferred to St Brelade's cemetery. The tower on the islet was built over the grave in 1808 as one of the many fortifications against possible invasion during the Napoleonic Wars.

From Portelet, return to the small crossroads, turn left and then take the right fork down to ★★ **Ouaisné Bay** (pronounced *Waynay*). The Smugglers' Inn, on the left as you go down, is evidence of former activities in this corner of the island. The magnicent sweep of beach, sheltered between headlands, stretches for over a mile, Ouaisné Bay being divided from St Brelade's by a rocky promontory called the Pointe le Grouin. Even on hot days in high season, Ouaisné's fine sandy beach has plenty of space.

The cliffs south of the bay shelter La Cotte de St Brelade (closed to the public), a major archaeological site where teeth of Neanderthal man and the bones of prehistoric beasts were discovered (*see Culture, page 59*). Behind Ouaisné beach, the gorse-covered common is home to some rare species of fauna, including the Dartford warbler, the Jersey green lizard and the agile frog; but sightings are rare. The German anti-tank wall, stretching the length of the beach, was built by prisoners during the German Occupation. Portelet Common, an expanse of heathland above the beach, commanding splendid coastal views, can be reached by the cliff path.

St Brelade's and Ouaisné Bay

★★ **St Brelade's Bay** is accessible by foot either across the sands or over the rocky promontory, depending on the tides. To reach the beach by car, return to the junction with the corner shop, turning left on to the A13, then

Tea on the seafront

fork left on to the B66 and descend to the bay. With its gently sloping, golden sands, sheltered setting and clear, blue waters, St Brelade's is justifiably the most popular beach on the island. Above the sands, the sea-front promenade is bordered by palm-lined gardens, cafés, hotels and gift shops. On the slopes above the bay lie some highly desirable tax-exile residences, surrounded by manicured gardens.

At the western end of the bay, the picturesque ★★ **Church of St Brelade** sits on a rocky ledge, overlooking the little harbour. Built of pink granite boulders from the shore, the church dates back to the 12th century and still retains its Norman chancel. Step inside and switch on the lights to reveal the enchanting interior with its warm, granite walls and intimate atmosphere. Pebbles from the beach are embedded in the unrendered granite and the occasional limpet still clings to the roof.

Fisherman's Chapel

Beside the church, the unique little ★★ **Fisherman's Chapel** is the oldest place of worship on the island, dating from the 11th–12th centuries, and built on the foundations of an older sanctuary. The chapel escaped destruction during the Reformation, and was variously used as an armoury, a store room for the sexton, a carpenter's shop and a meeting room. It was not until 1880 that permission was given for it to revert to a church. Restoration early in the 20th century brought to light the fragments of a series of beautiful medieval frescoes (1375–1425) decorating all four walls. These were restored in 1980 and today the scenes from the Old and New Testaments can be made out with the help of drawings on information boards which reconstruct the missing outlines. Clearest of all is the scene of the *Annunciation* on the east wall. The small kneeling figures either side of the Virgin and Archangel – seven

Annunciation fresco

Church of St Brelade

La Corbière cliffs and lighthouse

males to the left and seven females to the right – are members of the donor's family.

The flight of granite steps linking the churchyard with the small harbour is the shortest Perquage (sanctuary path) on the island. Before the Reformation, criminals who sought refuge in any of the parish churches were allowed to escape via such paths to the safety of a boat and sanctuary in France.

Take the steep road opposite the main entrance of the churchyard and then turn left for ★★ **Beauport**. This delightfully unspoilt bay is a favourite among islanders and smart yachts are often moored here on summer weekends. However, the climb down the hill and the absence of facilities on the beach deter most tourists, and it is seldom crowded during weekdays. If you are going to spend any time here – and it is a delightful place for swimming, snorkelling and sunbathing – take ample refreshments and a sunhat.

Leaving Beauport, turn left at the T-junction, and after ½ mile (1km) left again on to the B83 Route du Sud for ★★ **La Corbière**. Meaning haunt of the crow *(corbeau)*, traditionally a bird of ill omen, this is a wild and desolate corner of the island, abounding in tales of shipwrecks. The first recorded disaster involved a Spanish vessel carrying a cargo of wine in 1495. Many other boats have foundered here, including the Royal Mail Steam Packet in 1859, with loss of many lives.

However, it was not until 1874 that a lighthouse, the first in the British Isles to be made of concrete, was built here. Perched on jagged rocks and surrounded by some of the roughest seas in the Channel, this makes a dramatic scene at any time of day. There are still occasional accidents here, the most recent involving a French catamaran, en route from Jersey to Sark, which struck a rock north of the lighthouse in 1995. The sculptured pair of clasped hands on the headland commemorates the rescue of all 307 passengers and crew.

At half-tide you can cross the causeway to the lighthouse but the incoming sea is treacherous, so it is advisable to be aware of tide patterns. A carved stone on the causeway recalls the fate of an assistant lighthouse keeper who drowned while trying to save a visitor stranded by the incoming tide. Nowadays a siren warns visitors when the tide approaches the causeway. Originally manned by four keepers, the lighthouse today is remotely operated and there is no access inside for visitors. During the Occupation, the Germans built bunkers at La Corbière and a massive observation tower to the east, which has been converted to self-catering accommodation. The look-out penthouse at the top of the tower provides a terrific 360° panorama of the island.

For ★★ **St Ouen's Bay** to the north, continue around the headland, passing above the rocky Petit Port Bay, and in about a mile turn left on to the B35. The longest bay in the Channel Islands, the swathe of sands stretches in a great 4-mile (6-km) arc, all the way from La Pulente in the south to L'Etacq in the north. Throughout the year surfers make the most of the huge rollers on the incoming tides. Surf boards, boogy boards and wet suits can be hired at various points along the beach or, for those who prefer to sit and watch, the sea wall affords shelter and there are occasional cafés above the beach with seaview terraces (Big Vern's is the best bet for breakfast, lunch and sunset suppers). All but experienced surfers should heed the danger warnings and keep to the areas between the flags where lifeguards are on duty during summer. La Pulente at the southern end is protected from the Atlantic swell and, if the tide is not high, there are sandy pools in the rocky outcrops which young children can enjoy.

At the southern end of the bay **La Rocco** tower, dating from the turn of the 18th century, is the oldest of nine towers which were built to defend the bay during the Napoleonic Wars. Damaged by Germans target shooting during the Occupation, the tower underwent renovation in 1969. Only three of the other towers survive, one of them, **Kempt Tower**, being a fine example of a Martello tower (1834). This has been converted into a **Visitors' Centre** (May–Sept daily 2–5pm), which contains informative displays on **Les Mielles Conservation Zone**. Exhibits cover landscape, ecology, history and prehistory, including information on the prehistoric relics among the sand dunes. The conservation area, which is the largest remaining area of unspoilt countryside on the island, is noted for its extensive sand dune system.

In autumn and winter tractors load up with *vraic* (pro-

St Ouen's Bay

31

La Rocco Tower

Traditional knitwear for sale

Life in a bunker at the Channel Islands Military Museum

nounced 'rack') or seaweed from the beach for use as a fertiliser on the farmland bordering the coast. Horses and carts were once used for the job, gaining access to the beaches via slipways which you can see all the way around the Jersey coastline. In 1600 laws were passed to guarantee farmers equal rights to the free fertiliser. Today it is a free-for-all.

The beach is skirted by the confusingly named Five Mile Road – it is actually only 3 miles (4.5km) long. Follow this north, to the end of the main beach for the **Jersey Woollen Mills**. Knitting is one of the islands' oldest traditions and records date back to the 16th century when women would knit sweaters to keep their menfolk warm on their long journeys to the cod banks in Newfoundland. Men knitted too and the manufacture of jerseys became so popular that in 1608, in order to encourage more workers onto the land, an act was passed prohibiting anyone over the age of 15 from knitting during harvest time. The penalty was imprisonment. Each jersey made on the Channel Islands had its own distinctive style and legend has it that if a sailor was lost at sea and his body washed ashore, he would be identified by his sweater and retuned to his native parish. The sweaters sold here are in fact made in Alderney with wool imported from the UK.

Close to the shore lies the ★ **Channel Islands Military Museum** (late Mar–early Oct, daily 10am–5pm), housed in a restored German bunker which once formed part of Hitler's Atlantic war defences. The museum is packed with Occupation memorabilia, British as well as German. Military and civilian exhibits include soldiers in uniform, military motorcycles, a rare Enigma decoding machine, Red Cross letters to relations and friends in England (limited to 25 words) and Christmas and birthday cards made by Jersey internees at Worzach and Bieberach camps in southern Germany.

Another tourist attraction of a rather different nature is **Jersey Pearl**, just across the main road. Here you can watch pearl threading, have your own necklace made or choose from a wide range of cultured, freshwater or simulated pearls.

The main road heads inland after Jersey Pearl. The B35 takes you to L'Etacq, a vast expanse of reefs better suited to rockpool exploring than swimming. The old German bunker at the far end sells lobster, crabs, prawns and fresh fish. For a gourmet picnic, order lobster ready cooked (Faulkner Fisheries, tel: 01534 483500).

From L'Etacq you can continue up to Grosnez *(see Route 4, page 43)*. The main road inland (B64) brings you to the village of **St Ouen**. Behind the Parish Hall on the far side of the A12, and marked off the road, is the **Bouchet Agateware Pottery** (daily 9am–5pm, www. agateware.co.uk), where Tony Bouchet produces a wide range of pottery in the style of semi-precious stone (agateware). Although agateware has been produced in the past (and notably by ancient Chinese potters), Tony Bouchet's work is unique in its wide range of colours, and this is the only agateware pottery in existence today. The process, which has taken him decades to perfect, remains a closely guarded secret.

The ★ **parish church of St Ouen's**, one of the finest on the island, lies southwest of the actual village, on the crest of a hill overlooking the sea. To get there take the C117 marked to the right of the A12. The church was mentioned in a charter signed by William the Conqueror prior to his conquest of England. Major alterations and extensions took place between the 12th and 19th centuries. The original building, possibly a chantry chapel built by 7th-century monks from Normandy, is thought to have been rebuilt or enlarged by a member of the historic de Carteret family, Seigneurs of St Ouen, whose nearby ancient seat can be seen from the main A12. The Manor of St Ouen (closed to the public), owned by the family for over 800 years, was used by Germans during the Occupation and St Anne's chapel was turned into a storeroom and butcher's shop.

The next village along the A12 is St Peter's, whose parish church has the tallest spire on the island and hence a warning red light for planes. A church has stood on this site for well over 1,000 years. Like St Ouen's, it predates the Conquest.

Return to St Helier by continuing south along the A12 and turning left on to the A1.

Fresh crab at L'Etacq

33

Helmets at the Military Museum

Jersey Lavender: a blaze of colour

Route 3

Flowers and Farming

Waterworks Valley – Hamptonne Country Life Museum – La Mare Wine Estate – Moulin de Quétivel – Lavender Farm – Eric Young Orchid Foundation
See map, pages 24–5

Tea at La Mare Wine Estate

Although agriculture is no longer a main source of income for Jersey, farming is still a way of life for the islanders. Over a third of the land is agricultural and the sunny south-facing slopes yield Jersey Royal potatoes and tomatoes, while the famous doe-eyed Jersey cow provides islanders with milk, cream and butter. Flowers are grown both for export worldwide and for the decoration of the floats at Jersey's celebrated Battle of Flowers *(see page 62)*. The island is also famous for its orchids, both wild and cultivated, as well as other species of rare wild flowers. This route takes you into the heart of rural Jersey to a Country Life Museum and a wine estate, followed by a watermill and lavender farm and, finally, a detour to see some orchids.

From St Helier follow the signs for 'The West', taking you along the Esplanade. This becomes Victoria Avenue, venue of the annual Battle of Flowers which takes place every August and features bands, celebrities and a long parade of spectacular floats made of flowers. Apart from breaks during World War I and the German Occupation, the event has taken place every year since 1902 when the first 'Battle' celebrated the Coronation of King Edward VII. A day or two before the event volunteers can be seen busily cutting blooms and glueing them to the floats, though these days many are made of paper flowers. If you happen to miss the Battle, some of these amazing creations can be seen displayed around the parishes for a few days following the event.

When the road divides, follow the signs for the A1 which take you along the inner coastal road. Keep to this road until you see a turning to the right with a small sign for ★ **Waterworks Valley** (C118). The stream along this peaceful, green valley used to power six watermills – hence the name of the road 'Le Chemin des Moulins.' The late 19th century saw the construction of the 3-mile (4.5km) long Millbrook reservoir, followed later by the Dannemarche and Handois reservoirs to the north, giving the valley its somewhat pedestrian name.

Beyond the Dannemarche Reservoir, where the road forks, turn left on to the C119 for the ★★ **Hamptonne Country Life Museum** (Apr–Oct, daily 10am–6pm; tel: 01534 863955). This group of farmhouses and outbuildings in the heart of the countryside has been faithfully renovated to demonstrate 300 years of the island's rural heritage. The interiors of the two oldest houses have been recreated to illustrate living conditions of farming families in the 17th and 18th centuries. A third building is devoted to an informative exhibition demonstrating the changes in farming over the past 100 years and the decline in the island's agriculture – from 2,600 farms in the 1880s to just 500 today. At one end of the building the apple crusher and press are still used in the autumn to make cider. The restored outbuildings comprise stables, carriage house, bakehouse, wash house and farm labourers' accommodation.

Hamptonne Country Life Museum: cider press

This is very much a living museum with a farmer's wife (*goodwyf* in Jèrriais; *see page 8)* to tell you all the latest gossip from the 17th-century farming community or take you on a guided tour; there are also animals in the farmyard, demonstrations of bygone skills, a woodland path, wild flower garden and pond. The Hamptonne café make their own bread and cakes, as well as local specialities such as Jersey bean crock and Jersey Wonders. If you are here at lunch time, hampers can be ordered for picnics in the apple orchard.

Descending the road from the museum, turn right at the junction, then left and first right down a very narrow lane for the A10. Turn right and at the Carrefour Selous junction bear left on to the B39 for **Lion Park** (open all year 10am–5pm; www.jerseygoldsmiths.com). There are various gold and jewellery outlets here, including **Jersey Goldsmiths**; gold prices here are VAT-free and cheaper than those in the UK, but it is worth comparing them with

Hamptonne guide

the goldsmiths in St Helier before you buy. You can watch the craftsmen at work, commission a piece of jewellery to be designed, see the Celebrity Memorabilia Exhibition, go boating on the lake or relax in the 12 acres (5 hectares) of parkland, surrounded by swans and flamingos.

Wine tasting at La Mare

Continue along the B39 towards St Mary's village and then follow the signs to the Devil's Hole and ★ **La Mare Wine Estate** (Easter–Oct, Mon–Sat 10am–5pm; www.lamarevineyards.com). Centring around an old granite farmhouse, the vineyard comprises 12 acres (5 hectares) of vines, orchards and gardens. The estate now produces a wide range of ciders, red, white and sparkling wines, spirit and liquors. Guided tours of the vineyards, winery, distillery and chocolate factory include tastings along the way. Miniature ponies and an adventure playground keep youngsters entertained, and the popular Copperage restaurant and tearooms provide refreshments. Cream teas are, of course, made with the thick yellow cream from the Jersey cow.

Return to the main B33 in the direction of St Mary's Village and very shortly afterwards turn left on to the B26, signed to **St Peter's Valley**. This will join the A11 which runs through the valley. It was here that Queen Victoria was brought when she asked to see the most beautiful spot on the island. The valley was the site of six water mills, used mainly for grinding flour.

A mill with history

Turn right on to the B58, just over a mile along the A11, to see the only surviving mill on Jersey, the ★★ **Moulin de Quétivel** (Tues, Wed and Thur in season, 10am–4pm). A mill has operated here intermittently since feudal times, the current one dating from the 18th century. Abandoned in the early 20th century, it was revived by the Germans during the Occupation, only to fall into disrepair again. It was eventually brought back to working order by the National Trust in 1979. The top floor has an exhibition on the history of milling, while the first and ground floors demonstrate how the mill works. There is also a video which shows you how cabbage loaves (still sold in some bakeries on the island) are made in gorse ovens. The stoneground flour which at the mill is sold in the ground-floor shop. An attractive footpath, through woodland, runs from the mill to the mill-pond.

Continuing on the B58, go straight over the next crossroads for the A12. Turn left here and right at the roundabout which bypasses the airport and brings you into St Brelade. Just after the Quennevais shopping precinct turn left along the B25, signposted to ★ **Jersey Lavender** (May–Sept, Tues–Sun 10am–5pm). The fields of lavender, covering 9 acres (4 hectares), provide a Provençal-

Harvest time at Jersey Lavender

like blaze of purple throughout the summer. The *lavandage* or lavender harvest is usually over by mid-August but visitors can still watch the distilling and bottling processes and purchase oils and lotions made from the lavender essence. Further attractions are the herb garden, woodland walk and tea room.

To return to St Helier, continue along the B25 until you reach the coast road at St Aubin's. The A1 will bring you back into town. Alternatively you could end the route at St Ouen's Bay (easily reached from St Brelade via the A13 and B35), where some of the island's rarest species of flora are found *(see Route 2, page 31)*.

Jersey Lavender gardens

Detour to Eric Young Orchid Foundation

Floral enthusiasts should not leave Jersey without a visit to the ★ **Eric Young Orchid Foundation** (Wed–Sat, 10am–4pm; www.ericyoungorchidfoundation.co.uk), northeast of St Helier. From the town take the ring road, following signs to 'The North', then turn off for the A8 to Trinity. After half a mile, turn right, following signposts for Les Grands Vaux and the Orchid Foundation. The road takes you past Les Grands Vaux reservoir, then to Victoria village, where the Foundation is signposted to the left.

37

The late Eric Young devoted his life to breeding new hybrids of orchid and his exhibitions won prestigious awards. He first established a collection in Jersey in 1958 and within a decade it was recognised as one of the leading private collections in Europe. Young's ambition to set up an orchid foundation open to the public was achieved, but he died in 1984 at the age of 73 before the project was completed. The fruits of his lifelong efforts can be seen in the growing houses and the display area where orchids of dazzling colours are set against a backdrop of ponds, branches, rocks and raised beds.

Eric Young orchids

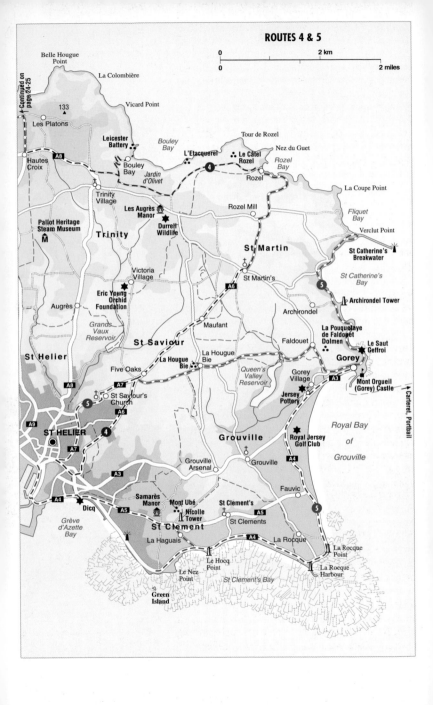

ROUTES 4 & 5

0   2 km

0   2 miles

Belle Hougue Point

La Colombière

Vicard Point

Continued on page 24-25

133

Les Platons

Leicester Battery

Bouley Bay

L'Etacquerel

Tour de Rozel

Le Câtel Rozel

Nez du Guet

4

Hautes Croix

A8

Bouley Bay

Jardin d'Olivet

Rozel

Rozel Bay

La Coupe Point

Trinity Village

Rozel Mill

Fliquet Bay

Les Augrès Manor

Durrell Wildlife

Rozel Mill

Verclut Point

Pallot Heritage Steam Museum

M

Trinity

St Catherine's Breakwater

St Martin

Victoria Village

St Martin's

St Catherine's Bay

5

Eric Young Orchid Foundation

A6

Archirondel Tower

Augrès

Archirondel

Grands Vaux Reservoir

Maufant

La Pouquelaye de Faldouet Dolmen

Le Saut Geffroi

St Saviour

Faldouet

St Helier

La Hougue Bie

La Hougue Bie

Gorey

Five Oaks

Queen's Valley Reservoir

Gorey Village

A8

5

St Saviour's Church

A7

Jersey Pottery

Mont Orgueil (Gorey) Castle

A6

A3

A9

4

Carteret, Portbail

ST HELIER

A7

Grouville

Royal Jersey Golf Club

Royal Bay

of

Grouville

A3

Grouville Arsenal

Grouville

A4

A4

Fauvic

A5

Dicq

Samarès Manor

Mont Ubé

St Clement's

5

Grève d'Azette Bay

Nicolle Tower

St Clements

La Rocque

A4

A5

La Haguais

A4

La Rocque Point

St Clement

Le Hocq Point

La Rocque Harbour

Le Nez Point

St Clement's Bay

Green Island

Route 4

Rozel Bay

The North Coast

Rozel Bay – Bouley Bay – Bonne Nuit – Devil's Hole
– Grève de Lecq – Plémont – Grosnez Castle *See map
opposite and on pages 24–5*

This glorious coast should ideally be covered on foot *(see page 52)*, but it can also be admired from bays which are accessible by car. Alternatively, the bays can be used as a base for short sections of the 15-mile (24-km) north coast footpath. The route starts at Rozel Bay in the east, winds over the cliffs, dips down to sandy bays and ends at Grosnez Point at the northwesterly tip of the island. Allow a whole day for all the diversions, take a picnic lunch or stop at a simple café for freshly caught seafood. (The Hungry Man Café at Rozel does a fabulous crab sandwich.)

Fishermen's huts and cafés

From the St Helier ring road follow the signs for 'The North' and the Five Oaks roundabout. From here take the A6 to St Martin's, then the B38 to ★ **Rozel Bay**. Tucked away in the northeast corner of the island, this is a small picturesque bay where fishermen's huts, cottages and cafés overlook the tiny harbour and the sand, shingle and rock beach. The pier was built in 1829 during the heyday of the oyster industry. Overlooking the bay, Le Beau Couperon Hotel was originally barracks, built in 1810 at the height of the Napoleonic threat. Being the closest point in Jersey to France, Rozel was considered a valuable defence site. However, no shot was ever fired here in battle.

The lush **Rozel Valley**, approached from behind the village, makes a pleasant inland walk with its exotic trees and shrubs. Subtropical flora were first planted here

Pleasure craft at Bouley Bay

Wild flowers above the bay

Cliffs at Bouley Bay

by a 19th-century naturalist, Samuel Curtis, and some of them can still be seen today.

From Rozel return to the C93 and after 1½ miles (2km), turn right into Rue du Becquet. This joins the C95, and from here follow the signs for ★ **Bouley Bay**. As you near the coast the road snakes it way down through the wooded hillside to a pebble bay surrounded by high cliffs. The steeply shelving beach and the deepest waters around the island's shores are ideal for scuba diving. The **Bouley Bay Diving Centre** based below the Water's Edge Hotel offers lessons and facilities to divers of all standards, including 'try dives' for beginners. Bouley Bay is also the venue of the very popular spring and summer Hill Climbs, which take place up the steep road from the bay. Any member of the British Hill Climbing Assocation equipped with motorbike, saloon car, racing car, sports car or even a bike is welcome to participate. The village is otherwise peaceful, with no more to it than the hotel, a café above the beach and the **Black Dog** pub, named after the fictitious Black Dog of Bouley Bay *(see page 62)*.

On the east of the bay, perched above the sea and blending with the cliffs, the fort of **L'Etacquerel** was one of several defences built to guard the north coast from French invasions. Another was **Fort Leicester** to the west, reached up the steps to the left just before the jetty. Both forts have been converted into holiday accommodation. L'Etacquerel has basic 'stone tent' accommodation providing space for 30 overnight (with sleeping bags), while Fort Leicester is more comfortable, sleeping six and complete with spacious bathroom and sea-view balcony. Cliff paths either side of Bouley Bay provide delightful walks. In summer the hills are ablaze with heather and wild flowers, while shags, which nest in cliff crevices in the spring, can be seen flying close to the shore.

Leaving Bouley Bay, climb back up to the top of the hill and turn right at the T-junction along the Rue de la Petite Falaise to join the main A8. Take the next main right turn (B63) and follow the signs for Bonne Nuit. To the right **Les Platons**, at 420ft (140m) above sea level, is the highest spot in Jersey – hence the forest of TV and radio masts.

Ducks at Bonne Nuit Bay

The name ★ **Bonne Nuit** (Good Night) appears to have derived from the now non-existent Chapel of Bona Nochte, built in the 12th century. Conversely, the sea beyond the bay used to be called Maurepos (Bad Repose), possibly on account of smugglers. Today it is a secluded little bay, with a tiny harbour and a sand and shingle beach, sheltered below heather-clad hills. At low tide fishing boats and pleasure cruisers are beached on the sands, and resident ducks waddle across the bay, hoping for a crust from the Bonne Nuit beach café. The red wooden huts on the jetty belong to fishermen who go out daily for lobsters, crabs and clams and a notice on the small building near the café details the minimum size of each type of shellfish that can be taken out of the sea. In ancient times fishermen and other islanders rowed around Le Cheval Guillaume or Cheval Roc, the offshore rock, to protect them from evil spirits. Bonne Nuit pier is the finishing point for the Sark to Jersey Rowing Race, held every July, and a plaque, unveiled by Chay Blyth (who, with John Ridgeway, rowed the Atlantic in 92 days in 1966) commemorates the silver jubilee. The fastest rowers from Sark take about 2½ hours.

Exploring Jersey's beaches

On the promontory to the east of the bay **La Crête Fort**, built by the British in 1835 and extended during the German Occupation. Until recently it was the weekend retreat of the island's Lieutenant-Governor. Today it is let out as holiday accommodation and what it lacks in comfort is more than compensated for by the spectacular views.

The devil at Devil's Hole

From Bonne Nuit climb up the hill marked 'La Saline' (the C99), take the first lane on the right and, at the T-junction, turn left and almost immediately right for the very narrow Rue ès Nonnes. This meets the C100, also known as La Route du Nord, which was built by islanders during the German Occupation. As you head northwest you will see a sign to Sorel Point, the most northerly point in Jersey, commanding splendid views to the west. East of the headland Ronez Quarry is one of the very few blots on the northern coastline.

The main road now veers away from the coast and becomes a green lane. At the next crossroads turn right for Le Creux du Vis (Screw Hole) or, as it is more popularly known, ★ **Devil's Hole**. Park at the Priory Inn and take the steep footpath down the hill to see the yawning chasm in the cliff, created by the erosion of the roof of a former cave. Most visitors keep at a safe distance behind a concrete wall well above the hole, others scramble down

Grève de Lecq

to sea level and watch the waters crash through as the tide comes up. The melodramatic name was acquired in the 19th century and probably derives from the figurehead of a mid-19th-century French shipwreck, which was found here and crafted into a wooden horned devil. Over the years various replicas of the devil have been placed on the path down, but each one has been stolen. The latest one towers over the pond at the start of the path near the pub.

Going south from Devil's Hole, take the second road on the right, past the La Mare Wine Estate *(see Route 3, page 36)*. At the fork keep to the right for La Rue des Tourettes and turn left at the next fork for ★ **Grève de Lecq**. This very narrow one-way lane, dropping steeply to the bay, is a section of the north coast cliff path which veers inland to avoid the rifle range. Beware, therefore, of pedestrians. Sheltered by cliffs, with a sandy beach and rock pools, Grève de Lecq is the most popular bay on the north coast.

Cell at the Barracks

Behind the bay, the **Barracks** (May–Sept, Wed–Sat 10am–5pm, Sun 1–5pm) were built to house garrison troops in 1810 when the island feared a French invasion. The buildings, restored by the National Trust, include the North Coast Visitors Centre, devoted to the wildlife and history of the area. The exhibitions provide detailed panels on the north coast footpaths, scenes from military life in the barracks, displays on Grève de Lecq's past and a collection of horse-drawn carriages.

Moulin de Lecq

Further up the main road, the **Moulin de Lecq**, which has been turned into an inn, was formerly a water mill. The stream here, which gushes out on to the beach, is the dividing line betweeen the parishes of St Mary and St Ouen. The massive mill wheel, which provides a dramatic backdrop to the Moulin de Lecq bar, is still in working order, though it is no longer used for grinding.

Overlooking the bay to the east and reached along the coastal path, **Le Catel de Lecq** is believed to be the site of an Iron Age hill Fort. At the east end of the bay you can walk along the cliff path, via the deep **Venus' Pool**, to the long dark tunnel through the rocks to the otherwise inaccessible beach of Le Catel de Lecq. This is an exciting trip but one that can only be done at low tide, preferably with a local to show you the way.

The last beach on the north coast is ★ **Plémont**, or more correctly La Grève au Lançon (Sand-eel beach). To get there take the road uphill out of Grève de Lecq, turning right on to the B55, and right again at the small crossroads at Portinfer. Plémont beach to the north remains unspoilt thanks to the lack of vehicular access. Leave the car at the park above the bay and walk down the path and steps. Low tide reveals a wide expanse of fine sands, rock pools and a network of caves in the cliffs on the landward side; but at high tide the sea completely covers the beach. From the headland to the east, accessible by the North Coast footpath, you can sometimes see small numbers of puffins, razorbill and fulmars during the summer months.

Returning to Portinfer, rejoin the B55 for ★★ **Grosnez** (signed off the road), whose medieval castle ruins stand evocatively 200ft (60m) above the sea. The only recognisable feature is the Gothic arch, although the foundations of walls and buildings beyond it are clearly visible. A reconstruction on the information panel shows how the castle would have originally looked, complete with drawbridge, portcullis and machiolated upper storey. Nothing is known of the castle's history other than it was built in the 14th century and destroyed, probably by the French, either in the same century, or when they occupied Jersey in 1461–68. Carved corbels which once decorated the arch but fell off long ago can be seen in the Archaeological Museum at La Hougue Bie *(see Route 5, page 44).*

Grosnez Castle

43

Walk through the arch for fine views, weather permitting, of all the other Channel Islands. From left to right these are Guernsey, Jethou, Herm, Sark, and in the very far distance, Alderney. France lies in the distance to the east, while offshore, a chain of rocks known as **Pater Noster** (Our Father) is visible at low tide. The name originated from a shipwreck here, involving families who were on their way to colonise the then uninhabited island of Sark. Several of them were drowned, including women and children. Since then it has been customary for sailors and fishermen to recite the Lord's Prayer when passing the treacherous reef.

Ruins with a view

La Hougue Bie: the chamber

Route 5

Sights and Beaches of the East

St Saviour's Church – La Hougue Bie – Mont Orgueil Castle – St Catherine's Bay – Jersey Pottery – Samarès Manor *See map on page 38*

The route focuses on the the main sights in the east of the island: a prehistoric burial mound, a medieval castle and a manor house with attractions for all ages. Beaches north and south of the village of Gorey provide a pleasant break from sightseeing.

Take the St Helier ring road, following signs first for the north and then for the A7 to the Five Oaks roundabout. This will take you through the parish of St Saviour's, where Lillie Langtry *(see page 20)* was born. She was married twice in the **Church of St Saviour**, and is buried close to a beech tree in the churchyard. South of the church, Government House is the official residence of the Lieutenant-Governor, the Queen's representative on the island.

Lillie Langtry at St Saviour's

At the Five Oaks roundabout, turn right on to Princes Tower Road (the B28). At the next T-junction turn left for ★★ **La Hougue Bie** (late Mar–Oct, daily 10am–5pm; www.jerseyheritagetrust.com). This remarkable site, in the heart of the countryside, is dominated by a 40-ft (13-m) burial mound, covering a Neolithic ritual site, dating to about 3,500BC. The word 'Hougue' derives from the Norse *haugre* meaning a burial mound and the 'Bie' may be a corruption of the Norman family name of Hambye.

The mound at La Hougue Bie

One of the many legends surrounding the mound concerns the valiant Seigneur de Hambye who was called from France to slay the dragon of St Lawrence which was wreaking havoc amongst the islanders. He succeeded in his mission, but his squire, who had designs on the Seigneur's wife, murdered his master, and informed her that the dragon had mortally wounded her husband and that he himself was responsible for killing the creature. The seigneur's dying wish, he told her, was for his wife to marry the servant who had avenged his death. She agreed to marry the squire but the new Lord Hambye disclosed his guilt in his sleep. On discovering the truth Lady Hambye came to Jersey and buried her husband under a mound (La Hougue Bie), huge enough for her to see from the castle keep of Hambye (in Normandy).

Excavations under the mound in 1924 revealed a low passage leading to chambers made of huge stone blocks. Fragments of bone from eight bodies, flint tools, bones of sheep, pig and ox, beads, pottery and limpet shells were all discovered within the dolmen.

Neolithic axe

The pagan site was christianised by the construction of two medieval chapels on top of the mound. The oldest is Notre Dame de la Clarté, dating from the 12th century, but heavily restored. The Jerusalem Chapel, which preserves the faint outlines of two archangels, was built in 1520 by Dean Mabon who, according to puritanical sections of the church, made money by performing fake miracles in the church crypt. In the late 18th century the chapel ruins were transformed by the D'Auvergne family into a Neo-Gothic folly with a castellated wall and two towers. The Tour d'Auvergne, or Prince's Tower as it was known, was abandoned at the end of the 18th century but in the following century became a tourist attraction, offering panoramic views, a bowling alley and the Princes Tower Hotel.

45

Within the grounds of La Hougue Bie is a replica of a Neolithic house, a museum of archaeology with the bones and teeth of prehistoric animals discovered at La Cotte de St Brelade *(see Culture, page 59)*. A legacy of more recent history is the German command bunker at the foot of the mound housing a poignant exhibition dedicated to slave workers in the Channel Islands. The Germans also constructed a watchtower on top of the mound at the west end and 70 trenches within the grounds.

Turn right out of La Hougue Bie and follow the signs for ★ **Gorey** on the east coast. Nearing the village a steep road brings you down to that most famous of Jersey landmarks, ★★★ **Mont Orgueil Castle** (daily 10am–5pm, winter 4pm). Translated as Mount Pride, and also known as Gorey Castle or Le Vieux Château, this mighty fortress towers over the harbour and commands the entire east coast. It is an impressive site at any time of day, but particularly picturesque after dark in summer when the battlements are floodlit.

The castle was built on the orders of King John, after he had lost Normandy and the Channel Islands had decided to remain loyal to the British crown. During its long history, this impregnable fortress rarely succumbed to the successive attacks from the French. The notable exception was an invasion in 1461 when the fortress fell into the hands of the French for seven years. With the construction of Elizabeth Castle, designed to meet the demands of modern-day warfare, Mont Orgueil became redundant; and were it not for the intervention of Sir Walter Raleigh, who thought it a shame to lose such a 'stately fort', it would have been razed to the ground.

In the 17th and 18th centuries the castle played various roles: a stronghold of the Royalists in the English Civil War, a state prison under Cromwell, a refuge for French aristocrats and the headquarters of a spy network during the French Revolution. You can still see the chamber where William Prynne, the 17th-century puritan, began his sentence. Not only incarcerated, he had his ears cut off and the initials S.L. (Seditious Libeller) branded on his cheek. A fine example of a concentric castle, Mont Orgueil was sited on an Iron Age hill fort and designed with a series of independent defences, with walls going straight out of the rock.

Gorey by night and day

Following an extensive restoration programme the castle reopened in 2006; its new exhibition gives you an insight into the castle's history and its significance to the island over the past 800 years. The Living History programme provides a flavour of the medieval era, with daily demonstrations of skills of combat and weaponry, weaving and embroidery. Visitors can try their hand at archery, dress in medieval costume or learn how to train eagles.

A climb up the steep battlements to the 13th-century keep will be rewarded by stunning views. At the top of the castle the 16th-century **Somerset Tower**, adapted by the Germans as an observation post, commands superb views. France can usually be seen across the water and on a really clear day you can make out the power station at Cap de la Hague on the tip of the Cherbourg peninsula.

In the shadow of the castle lies the quaint harbour of **Gorey**, where shops, pubs and cafés cluster around the waterfront. The village developed in the early 19th century when the flourishing oyster industry gave Gorey the sobriquet of 'the pearl of the east'. In 1820 English fishing fleets invaded the coast to share in the profits but by the middle of the century the oyster beds had been over-dredged and the industry was all but over. Today the harbour protects a fleet of pleasure craft and, as the only official seaport in Jersey apart from St Helier, offers high-speed catamaran trips to the port of Carteret in Normandy. At the end of the pier in the ferry terminal you will find Gorey's Discovery Pier where you can learn about coastal wildlife, fishing and the Jersey tides.

The coast road north of Gorey, the B29, climbs up towards the rocky promontory known as Le Saut Geoffroi or **Jeffrey's Leap**, named after a convicted criminal and renowned womaniser who managed to survive unscathed after his punishment of jumping from the cliffs to the rocks below. He was declared a freed man but, eager to impress the fair sex, he decided to perform the feat again. This time, however, his luck ran out.

Just beyond Jeffrey's Leap, a narrow lane on the other side of the road leads up to ★ **La Pouquelaye de Faldouet**, a Neolithic dolmen *(see Culture, page 59)*.

The main road skirts the pebble and sandy bay of Anne Port, and follows the coast by the bay of Havre de Fer and past the distinctive red and white **Archirondel Tower**, built in 1874. Keep to the B29 for **St Catherine's Bay**, enclosed to the north by a ½-mile (1-km) long breakwater which was built as a result of a British blunder in the mid-19th century.

Archirondel Tower

In answer to a naval base at Cherbourg and other French coastal installations, the British Government chose this site (as well as one at Alderney) for a harbour. Despite warnings that the depth of water was insufficient and the harbour would silt up, the project nevertheless went ahead and breakwaters were built here and at Archirondel. Twenty years and £250,000 later, the project was abandoned. The St Catherine's arm of the harbour was preserved and a lighthouse built at the end.

Today the breakwater is popular for fishing and promenading. The coast road stops here, but you can get to Fliquet Bay to the north on foot.

The road going south from Gorey Harbour and skirting the Royal Bay of Grouville *(see page 48)* brings you to Gorey Village, where the chief attraction for tourists is the ★ **Jersey Pottery** (open all year, Mon–Sat 9am–5.30pm,

Lobster pots at St Catherine's Bay

Sun 9am–5pm; www.jerseypottery.com). This is a highly organised commercial enterprise, where visitors can watch at close hand all the processes of pottery production, from the raw clay stage to the decoration and glazing. At each stage there are information boards with clear explanations of the techniques used. The show room displays a large range of ceramic tableware and decorative pieces, including Jersey-themed pieces such as the bean crock, milking can and Jersey cow. The pottery has been producing ceramics for 50 years and exports to 20 different countries.

Skilled hands at Jersey Pottery

Gourmets come to the pottery for food alone: the Garden Restaurant serves some of the best seafood on the island *(see page 67 for contact details)*.

The Garden Restaurant

Continuing south, to the east of the main road lies the ★ **Royal Bay of Grouville**, which stretches for 3 miles (5km) between Gorey and La Rocque Point. Guarding the bay are a number of towers built as coastal defences in the second half of the 18th century. These fortifications were armed and manned, but never actually used to defend the island. Queen Victoria, so impressed by this long and spacious sandy bay, gave it the Royal prefix after her visit in 1859. Shortly on the left are the links of the **Royal Jersey Golf Club**, the most exclusive on the island.

The route returns to St Helier via the coast road (A3 and A4), stopping at the little harbour of **La Rocque** in the southeastern corner of the island. It was here that Baron de Rullecourt and his troops secretly landed in January 1781, en route to their defeat at Royal Square in St Helier *(see Route 1, page 17)*. Low tide reveals a huge expanse of reefs and gullies, and Seymour Tower, standing on a rocky islet 2 miles (3km) to the southeast, can be reached

Royal Bay of Grouville

on foot. Beware, however, of the large tidal flow and the rapid incoming waters: the sea can rise 18 inches (50 cm) in 10 minutes. The tower, which has stood guard over the island since 1782, lies 1½ miles (2km) offshore, and is reached over a vast wilderness of gullies, sandbars and rockpools. For the adventurous there is now the opportunity of staying at the tower overnight. Access is restricted to specific days, dependent on the tides, and all groups must be accompanied by an accredited guide (for further information visit www.jerseyheritagetrust.org).

From La Rocque continue on the A4, detouring briefly after 2½ miles (4km) at **Green Island**, a small rocky outcrop covered in grass (hence the name), accessible by foot if the tide is not too high. Prehistoric graves, along with human and animal bones, were discovered here in 1911, but were removed for safekeeping to the Jersey Museum. The island has been gradually eroded by the sea and restorers are currently trying to prevent it from being washed away. On the waterfront the Green Island Restaurant is one of the best places on the island for freshly caught fish and seafood.

Directly north, off the A5, lies ★★ **Samarès Manor** (Easter to mid-Oct, daily 9.30am–5pm; www.samares manor.com). The highlight of the parish of St Clement, the manor house has 14 acres (6 hectares) of beautifully landscaped gardens, with a Japanese garden, ponds with swans and ducks, an ancient dovecot and a delightful walled garden full of culinary, cosmetic and medicinal herbs.

The manor house, which is still a private home, can be visited on guided tours, as can the Jersey Rural Life and Carriage Museum, and there are weekday talks on plants and gardening. The name derives from the Old Norman French *Salse Marais,* or salt water marsh, dating from ancient times when the owners profited from the saltpans on the low-lying land to the south.

Among the plants grown here are the Jersey Kale or Long Jacks, the six-foot tall cabbages *(choux)* which were grown all over the island in the 19th century. Used for *soupe aux choux,* boiled with potatoes and lard, they also served as cross rafters, bean poles, cow fodder, fuel and for the well-known Jersey cabbage loaf *(see page 65).*

St Clement's best-known resident was Victor Hugo, who lived here for three years after his exile from France. In 1855 he was expelled from Jersey for his support of newspaper articles discrediting Queen Victoria for making a state visit to Paris. The next 15 years of his life were spent on Guernsey. A plaque on the side of a large rock at **Le Dicq** slipway commemorates the spot where Hugo delivered orations to his fellow exiles. Le Dicq, situated south of Howard Davis Park in St Helier, can be reached by taking the coastal route (A4) back to the capital.

49

Japanese garden at Samarès Manor

Woodturning display

One of the famous lowland gorillas

Feathered friends

Gerald Durrell and his wife, Lee

Durrell Wildlife

Les Augrès Manor, Trinity (tel: 01534 860000)
Open daily except Christmas Day, 9.30am–6pm, 5pm winter.

Headquarters of the Durrell Wildlife Conservation Trust, the ★★★ **Zoo** was founded by author and naturalist Gerald Durrell (1925–95) in 1963 and today is internationally renowned as a sanctuary and breeding centre for some of the world's most endangered species. This is no ordinary zoo. 'The idea behind my zoo was to aid in the preservation of animal life,' Durrell wrote, 'to build up under controlled conditions breeding stocks… so that, should the worst happen and the species become extinct in the wild state, you have, at least, not lost it forever. Moreover, you have a breeding stock from which you can glean the surplus animals and reintroduce them into their original homes at some future date.' At Durrell's memorial service, Sir David Attenborough spoke of the zoo's priorities, which entailed putting 'the animals first, the staff second and the public as privileged paying guests'.

Breeding programmes have been developed with the Trust working in close cooperation with the governments and trainees of the native countries of the endangered species. More than 300 trainees from 70 different countries have studied at the International Training Centre for the Captive Breeding and Conservation of Endangered Species, started up with funds raised by the Trust's US sister organisation and opened in 1984 by the Trust's patron, the Princess Royal. Many of the animals are the last survivors of their species and the zoo is their only chance of survival. The Trust continues to fulfil Durrell's ambition to reintroduce animals bred in captivity to their native habitat.

Among the success stories are the pink pigeons bred in Jersey and reintroduced to the forests of Mauritius, the golden lion tamarins which have been released in a private reserve in Brazil, and the thick-billed parrots, considered extinct in Arizona, which are now flying free in their native pinewoods. Other species that have been pulled back from the brink are the Assam pygmy hog, the St Lucia whiptail lizard and the Mallorcan midwife toad. In 1989 a pair of St Lucia parrots flew courtesy of British Airways back to the Caribbean, accompanied by the Prime Minister of St Lucia who travelled to Jersey especially to escort them home.

Golden-headed lion tamarin and endangered reptile

Over thirty acres (12 hectares) of parkland and water-gardens, with rare flowers, shrubs and trees, are the setting for this exotic collection of mammals, birds and reptiles. Throughout the zoological park the Trust has tried, wherever possible, to cultivate the native habitat of the animals' wildlife. Compared to most zoos, the enclosures are spacious and imaginative, providing natural environments for family groups of endangered species.

Favourite inmates are the Sumatran orang-utans who provide endless entertainment in their splendid habitat of islands and waterways, the rare reptiles from Round Island, Mauritius, the marmosets and tamarins living free in the woodlands, the Livingstone fruit bats, with a wingspan of 6ft (almost 2m) and – most famous of all – the lowland gorillas. Beside the compound a statue commemorates Jambo, the mighty gorilla who hit the headlines in 1986 when he protected a 5-year-old boy who fell into the enclosure. The 'gentle giant', who fathered 13 offspring and died in 1992, was the first male gorilla to be reared in captivity. Today the big boss of the compound is the 35-stone (225-kg) Ya Kwanza.

Jambo

A moated enclosure near the entrance is home to a family of ring-tailed coatis and a much-loved and long-established pair of Andean bears, Wolfgang and Barbara. The only bears in South America, the Andean species is being pushed to extinction by the destruction of their natural habitats and the huge demand for bear blood, bile and organs used in traditional medicine and delicacies such as bear paw soup. A glass-domed interpretation centre, semi-submerged into the landscape, gives access to the enclosure and provides a 'behind-the-scenes' opportunity to demonstrate the role and techniques of breeding endangered species.

Admission tickets come with a map, information on daily talks (every half hour 11am–3pm) and feeding times. For further information, visit the Trust's website, www.durrell.org.

Drama along the north coast

Walking on Jersey

LA VALLETTE WALK

To experience the beauty of rural Jersey and the undeveloped stretches of coastline, there is no better way than to walk. The island may be small, but it offers some surprisingly dramatic and varied scenery, particularly along the northern coastline. The rural interior offers walks through woodlands, along valleys, reservoirs and through leafy lanes with granite farmhouses and cottages. In addition to footpaths there are 45 miles (72km) of Green Lanes, where the speed limit is a sedate 15 mph (24km/h), giving priority to pedestrians and cyclists. These roads are well signed with a special logo at the beginning and end of each lane. Other roads on the island tend to be busy in season and are best avoided by walkers. The network of footpaths continues to grow as the States open up new stretches, both along the coast and inland, often in conjunction with the Jersey National Trust and other landowners.

Jersey Tourism produces an excellent brochure on specialist guided walks, taking in the island's history, heritage, flora and fauna. These range from marine myths and legends, through coastal fortifications, ghost walks to hikes along cliff-top paths. The best map is the Jersey Ordnance Survey 1:25,000, which marks every footpath, boundary and building. When exploring the coast, visitors should watch out for extreme tidal movement, one of the largest recorded in the world. During the third and fourth hours of a rising spring tide, the rate of rise can be as much as 2½ inches (5cm) a minute. Tide tables are available from shops, and are also posted in the *Jersey Evening Post*.

At low tide 'moon walks' take place along the lunar-like seascape, between the southeast coast and Seymour Tower (for details visit www.jerseywalkadventures.co.uk). For more information and routes for self-guided walks that

From bay to bay

you can download visit the Jersey Tourism website: www.jersey.com/walking.

North coast

The north coast footpath offers mile after mile of majestic cliffs and dramatic rugged scenery. This is easily the most exhilarating walk on the island and one that can either be done in its entirety over a very long day, or preferably in separate sections at a gentler pace. The walk can be done at any time of year, but the scenery is at its best in spring when sea campion, thrift, ox-eye daisies, pennywort and bluebells are in full bloom. This is also the time of year when you might spot the Glanville fritillary butterfly dancing over the cliffs. Before undertaking the walk it is worth paying a visit to the North Coast Visitor Centre at the Barracks at Grève de Lecq.

Feeding time

Grosnez Point

The official footpath, a good deal of which was constructed by Jersey prisoners in the 1980s, runs almost the entire length of the north coast, all the way from Rozel in the northeast to Grosnez in the northwest (you can actually start at the headland at La Coupe in the far northeast, but the going is tricky between here and Rozel). The path occasionally breaks from the coast, diverting through wooded slopes or fields, and in St John's Parish, it joins the main road following the coast before heading inland to avoid the only blot on the north coast seascape: the unsightly quarry at Ronez. Most of the time the route is well signed but a map is neverthless useful. The whole walk is 15 miles (24km) long and it can be done by taking No 3 bus from St Helier to Rozel (the path begins behind the village) and No 8 back from Grosnez.

One section at a time

Perhaps the most spectacular stretch is Bouley Bay (No 4 bus from St Helier) to Bonne Nuit (No. 4 bus). Timetables are available from the bus station in St. Helier – they are also published in some of the free holiday publications. Parts of the walk are quite steep, particularly as the path climbs up from the bays, but there is nothing which would really challenge an averagely fit adult. Benches at regular intervals enable you to rest and admire the views, there are also cafés and pubs at the small fishing harbours en route. The views are stunning all the way, and on a clear day you can see across to France. In the west the walk ends at the ruins of Grosnez castle, which stand above black sheer cliffs and command views to the north of the other Channel Islands.

For stopping points along the way, *see Route 4, page 39*, which covers the north coast by car.

West coast

Although it lacks the exciting cliff scenery of the north coast, the footpath skirting the wild and windswept St Ouen's Bay offers a bracing walk. Surfers provide plenty of entertain-

Pond life

Corbière lighthouse

ment and there are occasional cafés along the way which make the most of the views. Conspicuous landmarks along the bay are the coastal defence towers: La Petite Tour or Lewis Tower, Kempt Tower (now a Visitor Centre) and the offshore La Rocco Tower to the south, all erected as defences against the French from 1778 to 1835. Behind the beach the sand dunes of Les Mielles Conservation Zone and the pond of St Ouen are a haven for naturalists *(see Route 2, page 31)*. Leaflets on the flora and fauna of the area are available from the Visitors' Centre at Kempt Tower, and bird buffs can fill in a checklist of 72 birds to be seen in Les Mielles. Exploration in the sand dunes here will also reveal Neolithic menhirs and the relics of more recent history in the foundations of 40 purpose-built huts which accommodated over 1,500 German prisoners during World War I. To the south of St Ouen's Bay, Corbière lighthouse can be reached by causeway if the tide is not high *(see Route 2, page 30)*. This is a favourite place to watch the sea and the sunset.

North of St Ouen's Bay the windswept clifftops between L'Etacq and Grosnez provide splendid views along the coastline. This walk can be done either as an extension of the north coast footpath, or as a short 3-mile (5-km) walk starting either at Grosnez or L'Etacq. Along the way the five-storey observation tower is a prominent *landmark on the clifftop and a coastal artillery battery (open most Saturdays from May to mid-September) has been carefully restored with gun emplacements and bunkers.

Further south, the 200-ft (60-m) high menhir-like rock known as The Pinnacle was an ancient ceremonial site, occupied in turn by Neolithic, Bronze Age, Iron Age and Roman settlers. The common here, called Les Landes, is the largest area of heath on the island, renowned for its wild open spaces and spectacular sea views. Exposed to Atlantic winds, it nevertheless supports a rich variety of wild plants and is strewn with gorse and heather in summer. It is also home to Jersey's racecourse, a rifle range and an airfield for model aircraft.

The southwest

The delightful southwest coast can be covered on foot, starting at Ouaisné Bay and ending at La Corbière. If the tide is high St Brelade's Bay can be reached from Ouaisné over the rocky promontory dividing the two beaches. At the far end of St Brelade's Bay, beyond the church above the tiny harbour, a path leads to the idyllic beach of Beauport. To reach the bay, you have to climb down the stepped path from the clifftop. From Beauport there is a path, though not always a very obvious one, along the rugged coastline to La Corbière. The scenery en route is not enhanced by the prison, radar station and desalination plant but these at least are useful landmarks. The route is otherwise scenic, affording some splendid coastal views.

For shorter strolls, Portelet Common, on the headland between Portelet Bay and Ouaisné Bay, commands stunning views over Ouaisné and St Brelade's Bay to the northwest and over Portelet Bay to the east. Noirmont Promontory, visible beyond Portelet Bay, and accessible by car, is not quite as scenic but nevertheless provides pleasant clifftop strolls and historic interest in its German Occupation relics *(see Route 2, page 27)*.

East coast

This is not Jersey's most exciting coast, and there are relatively few paths that follow close to the seashore. One of the worthwhile sections is the walk from Gorey to St Catherine's. (Bus No 1 or 1B will take you from St Helier to Gorey Pier, No 1B will bring you back from St Catherine's Bay). The route provides good views of the coast and on the way you can stop at Jeffrey's Leap and the Pouquelaye de Faldouet dolmen *(see Route 5, page 47)* and Archirondel beach, which makes a good spot for a picnic. The path from here takes you to St Catherine's Breakwater, a popular spot for anglers and promenaders. Off the approach road to the breakwater, an upper and a lower footpath lead to the rocky Flicquet Bay, which marks the end of the coastal path.

From this northeastern corner of the island there are good views of Les Ecréhous, the reef of rocks lying midway between Jersey and Normandy. In the early 14th century a prior, monk and one servant lived on Maître Ile, the largest of the reefs, and the remains of a small chapel can still be seen here. Today the islets are popular with sailors from Jersey and France.

From Gorey you can also walk southwards along the promenade to Grouville Common. Watch out here for stray golf balls because the common is home to the Royal

Sanctuary path at St Brelade's

Noirmont Point

Jersey Golf Club. Further south, there are steps in the sea wall which give access to the beach. At low tide you can walk right around the southeastern tip of the island, via La Roque and Le Hocq, to Green Island.

Inland walks

The most scenic inland walks focus on valleys and reservoirs. The path alongside Waterworks Valley, running north from Millbrook, follows the winding road past reservoirs and through wooded slopes. To the west, the Jersey War Tunnels is a good starting point for walks through attractive woodland along St Peter's Valley. In the northeast of the island, there are delightful walks in the thickly wooded valley of Rozel Woods, between St Catherine's Bay and St Martin's village. The path circling the Y-shaped Val de la Mare reservoir is an easy 3-mile (4.5-km) walk, providing fine views of the distant St Ouen's Bay from near the dam. Queen's Valley Reservoir, west of Gorey, provides another pleasant, undemanding walk which takes you around the trout-filled waters.

56

The railway walk

The now defunct Western Railway, linking St Helier with St Aubin, was extended to Corbière in 1884. Trains ran on a single line of standard-gauge track and, apart from delays caused by waves crashing over the sea wall along St Aubin's Bay, the service ran with remarkable efficiency. However, competition from buses and a fire at St Aubin's station led to the demise of the service in 1936. The track was turned into a footpath and today makes a delightful 4-mile (6-km) walk across the western corner of the island. The start of the path is signed off the main road as it turns inland from St Aubin's harbour. (Take bus Nos 12, 12A or 15 to St Aubin.)

There is no need for a map here – just follow the path until the end of the line. Along the latter part of the walk, the trees took a battering in the 1987 storm, but new ones have been planted. The railway line ended above Corbière, and the old station is now a private house. Corbière lighthouse can be reached along the causeway providing the tide is not too high. If you do not want to make the return journey on foot, the buses *(see above)* departing from the terminus will take you back to St Aubin or St Helier.

Seasonal walks

If you are here in spring or autumn don't miss the series of free guided walks during the third weeks of May and September. These are geared to all ages and abilities. In the third week of June keen hikers flock to Jersey for the Itex walk around the island. The distance is 48 miles (77km), taking 12–41 hours, with funds going to Jersey charities.

Cycling Tours

Along the green lanes

No distance on Jersey is too far to cycle and the network of quiet country lanes and coastal roads makes for pleasant, if at times strenuous, cycling.

A 96-mile (155-km) network has been established all over the island, and the clear signs along the way enable you to explore the winding lanes without constantly referring to maps. The routes take in the Green Lanes where pedestrians, cyclists and horse riders have priority over cars, and motorists must slow down to 15mph (24km/h). If a rural lane suddenly ceases to be a Green Lane, the probability is you have cycled across a parish boundary; two pro-car parishes (Trinity and St Saviour) are still resisting the Green Lane scheme.

57

Speed limit for cars

Visitors who want to plan their own cycling itineraries, should consult the Jersey Tourism website (www.jersey.com/cycling) for detailed cycling routes and the useful Jersey Cycling Map marking the coastal circuit, inland links and connections to various popular attractions.

The easiest introduction to a cycling holiday, particularly suitable for families with small children, is the designated footpath/cycle track following the old railway line above the bay from St Helier to St Aubin. The Railway Walk *(see facing page)* as far as La Corbière can also be used by cyclists.

For cycle hire, *see page 70*. For information on escorted, guided bike tours contact Jersey Cycle Tours, Old German Tunnels, Railway Path, St Aubin, tel: 01534 746780 or 482898. They operate Apr–Sept and provide reliable bikes for hire.

For those coming from the UK by sea, Condor Ferries (www.condorferries.com) will carry bicycles free of charge.

Cyclists in St Helier

Historic Landscape

Antiquity

Ancient tree stumps, visible very occasionally at St Ouen's Bay when the sand has been washed away by storms, are relics of a submerged prehistoric forest which existed before Jersey became an island. Originally forming part of the land mass of Europe, it broke away in around 6500BC, the last of the Channel Islands to do so. Palaeolithic man set foot on the island well over 100,000 years ago to hunt game and shelter in caves which were then many miles inland from the sea. Conspicuous evidence of their occupation are the human teeth, flint chippings and bones of mammoth and woolly rhinoceros discovered at La Cotte de St Brelade cave on the south side of Ouaisné Bay.

The first discoveries were made in 1881 but excavations continued on and off for another hundred years, revealing invaluable information about successive Palaeolithic hunters who lived here. Today the cave is considered one of the most important Palaeolithic sites in Europe. The mounds of animal bones found at the foot of the 98-ft (32-m) cliff suggested a specialised hunting technique whereby herds of prehistoric animals were stampeded to their death over the cliff edge. The cave is closed to the public, but relics, including teeth of Neanderthal man and the bones of animals, are on view in the Jersey Museum, St Helier *(see Route 1, page 19–20)* and in the museum at La Hougue Bie *(see Route 5, page 45)*.

Inside La Hougue Bie's chamber

Neolithic man, who arrived on the island over 6,000 years ago, left his mark in the monumental tombs and the standing stones which lie scattered around the island. The most impressive of the chambered tombs are the early passage graves or burial chambers, made of huge boulders and approached by a tunnel-like passage. These enigmatic monuments, often associated with fairies, played an important role in the rich folklore of the island. The most spectacular of these ancient sites is La Hougue Bie, a cruciform passage-grave whose huge mound was later crowned with two medieval chapels. La Pouquelaye de Faldouet, lying on a plateau inland from Gorey, is a long passage grave, badly damaged by diggers but nevertheless retaining an air of mysterious antiquity.

In 1785, during defence constructions on the hill now occupied by Fort Regent, an extensive dolmen was discovered resembling a mini Stonehenge. Since the grave was impeding construction of the fort, it was presented as a retirement present to General Conway, then Governor of the island. The mighty megaliths and capstones were shipped across the Channel and taken up the Thames to grace the general's private estate upstream from Henley-on-Thames, where the dolmen stands today.

The French wars

From 1204, when King John lost the English territories in France and the Channel Islands elected to remain loyal to the English crown, hostilities prevailed between the islands and France. Jersey was frequently threatened by invasions and fortifications were constructed, particularly along the vulnerable east coast, lying just 15 miles (24km) from Normandy. Mont Orgueil (Gorey Castle) was built overlooking Grouville Bay and remained the main stronghold on the island for nearly four centuries. This great medieval fortress withstood many attacks from the French, including a devastating raid in 1373 by the Constable of France, Bertrand du Guesclin, otherwise known as the Black Dog of Brittany. The castle fell just once in 1461, and a French force captured and held Jersey for the next seven years. By the end of the 16th century, Mont Orgueil could no longer withstand the attacks of modern warfare and Elizabeth Castle *(see Route 1, page 20)* was built on an islet in St Aubin's Bay.

Jersey's distinctive round towers (not to be confused with the later cam-shaped Martello towers) were built in the late 18th century as part of Governor Conway's plans to defend the coast against further possible invasion from the French. The lower storey served as a store for arms and provisions, the upper floor as accommodation for one officer and 10 men and the top of the tower as the gun platform. Towers and forts were built around the shoreline, particularly along the east and west coasts. The building programme was accelerated after the attempted French invasion in 1781 led by Baron de Rullecourt. The French were defeated at the Battle of Jersey, thanks to the gallant young Major Francis Peirson *(see page 18)*. Seymour Tower, unique among Jersey's coastal towers for its square plan form, was built in 1782 off La Rocque Point, where

60

BATTLE OF JERSEY
JANUARY 6TH 1781
THE FRENCH TROOPS UNDER THE COMMAND
OF BARON DE RULLECOURT
CAME ASHORE HERE

Officer's room in Elizabeth Castle

de Rullecourt had landed. In all, 31 coastal towers were built on the island, of which 24 survive.

By the early 19th century, with the collapse of peace after the Treaty of Amiens, Napoleon railed against Jersey as 'a nest of brigands', forcing the governors to improve the island's defences and construct a fortress on the hill above St Helier. Fort Regent was built in 1814, but was never used to defend the town. The Battle of Jersey was thus the last attempt by the French to attack the island.

German Occupation

In June 1940, after the evacuation of Normandy, the British Government reluctantly withdrew their troops from the Channel Islands. Ten thousand islanders were evacuated to England. On 1 July German planes dropped an ultimatum, demanding unconditional surrender. The Occupation of the islands – the only part of the British Empire captured by Hitler – began the following day and was to last for five years. Jersey, like Guernsey, was turned into an impregnable fortress, with thousands of foreign labourers used to construct coastal bunkers, continuous anti-tank walls, observation towers and artillery batteries. These concrete structures were left standing after the war as historic relics. Most evocative of all the German fortifications is the Jersey War Tunnels *(see page 22)* where slave labourers toiled in harrowing conditions to complete a huge complex of bomb-proof artillery barracks which was never actually used.

The German observation tower at Corbière is now holiday accommodation with a difference

For the islanders times were hard with rations, medicines and domestic fuel in short supply, particularly in the latter stages of the Occupation. A curfew was imposed, land requistioned, private vehicles confiscated, the sale of spirits banned and, worst of all, radio sets were confiscated. The rationing gave rise to ingenious substitutes for everyday comestibles such as acorn coffee, pea pod tea and roseleaf tobacco. In 1942 more than 1,000 British-born islanders were deported to Germany, the majority for political activities or for harbouring forbidden radio sets.

Following D-Day in June 1944, the Germans were cut off from mainland France, fuel was running out, and both islanders and occupiers were on starvation rations. In December the Bailiff appealed to the Red Cross and at the end of the month, the Swedish ship *Vega* arrived with 750 tons of Red Cross parcels. Five months later, on 8 May 1945, the message from Churchill was broadcast in Royal Square: '...and our dear Channel Islands are also to be freed today'. Liberation Square in St Helier – the spot were jubilant crowds greeted the British liberators – was opened on the 50th anniversary of that memorable day. The Liberation Sculpture, dominating the square, commemorates the event.

Liberation Square

Folkore and Festivals

Folklore

Jersey abounds with myth, superstition and strange customs. Prehistoric menhirs and dolmens gave rise to devil worship and witchcraft, and stormy seas sowed the seeds of legend. Many are the tales of the wreckers who lured ships onto the treacherous reef of Corbière by burning fires near the rocks, indicating a a safe haven from the stormy waters. The inevitable shipwreck would bring death to the crew and precious cargo to the fishermen. In medieval times the Seigneur of St Ouen was entitled to any booty washed ashore near his manor and there are records showing that in 1495 a cargo of wine from a Spanish shipwreck was plundered by the seigneur with the aid of parishioners. On the north coast tales were told of the Black Dog of Bouley Bay, a terrifying creature with huge saucer eyes that roamed the coastline of the bay. The dog in fact was an invention of smugglers who needed to frighten prying eyes away from the bay on the nights they landed their cargo. Other characters which contribute to Jersey legend are the dragon of St Lawrence which tormented villagers and La Pouquelaye, the fairy stone which gave its name to the mischievous 'Puck'.

Some islanders are still superstitious. Legend has it that cattle go down on bended knees on Christmas Eve and anyone who witnesses the animals worshipping will die before the year is out. Several of the old farmers still make sure their cattle are bedded well before the midnight hour.

Among Jersey's strange customs is *les visites du branchage*, a twice-yearly inspection by the parish Constable, Centeniers, Vingteniers, Road Committee and Road Inspectors to see that overhanging branches are not encroaching on roads and footpaths.

Battle of Flowers creation

Morris Men

Festivals

Jersey hosts various festivals throughout the year, the most celebrated of which is the **Battle of Flowers** *(see page 34)* held on the second Thursday in August. Attracting thousands of visitors, the parade features spectacular floats decorated with flowers and accompanied by marching bands, beauty queens headed by Miss Jersey and a celebrity Mr Battle. On the Friday evening selected floats and bands take part in the **Illuminated Moonlight Parade**.

Other flower, food and music festivals are hosted throughout the year (see www.jersey.com for exact dates). Popular events include the Jersey Live Music Festival in late August, billed as 'the biggest little Indie Rock festival in the British Isles', the International Air Display in September, and the Tennerfest (Oct–Nov) where for six weeks you can dine from £10 at over 100 restaurants.

Literature and the Arts

Lillie Langtry

Several famous literary and artistic figures have strong Jersey connections. The island's most famous painter was John Everett Millais (1829–96), a founder member of the Pre-Raphaelite brotherhood, who later became a fashionable painter of portraits, costume history and genre pieces. His painting of Lillie Langtry can be seen in the Jersey Museum *(see Route 1, page 19)*. The great French writer and political activist, Victor Hugo (1802–85), spent three years in Jersey following his exile from France in 1851. Modern-day Jersey attracts a different style of novelist, the most famous being Jack Higgins (real name Harry Patterson), author of *The Eagle Has Landed*.

Venues for theatre, music and the arts

In St Helier, the Jersey Arts Centre, Phillips Street (tel: 01534 700444; www.artscentre.je) offers a range of contemporary and classic performing and visual arts, including theatre, music, film and art exhibitions. After a £7.5 million restoration, the Jersey Opera House in Gloucester Street (tel: 01534 511115; www.jerseyoperahouse.co.uk) now hosts theatrical, musical and operatic productions. Its was built in 1900 on the site of the Theatre Royal, destroyed by fire the previous year. Lillie Langtry performed here on its opening night.

The Opera House

The Jersey Museum in St Helier has a gallery of 19th-century paintings of Jersey and hosts exhibitions of living local artists. In Trinity, the Jersey Heritage Trust Sir Francis Cook Gallery, Route de Trinité, opens for temporary exhibitions when visitors can also see the permanent collection of works by English artist Francis Cook (1907–78).

Food and Drink

Jersey has two culinary claims to fame: the uniquely flavoured Jersey royal potato and the rich, creamy milk from the Jersey cow. The delicious potatoes, which were first propagated in 1880, are ready for digging as early as April – well before the earliest new potatoes in the UK. Many are grown for export to the UK, but, for those who happen to be in Jersey in spring, there is nothing to compare with a new Jersey Royal straight from the soil.

For the islanders fishing has always been a way of life. In the Middle Ages the abundance of conger, which was salted, dried and shipped to England, led to the nickname 'Isle of the Congers', and from the 17th century, fortunes were made from the cod banks of Newfoundland. Boats still go out to lay the lobster pots and fish for bream, bass, cod, conger, monkfish, grey mullet and mackerel, but the shores have been overfished and species such as the indigenous ormer, prized for its unique flavour and mother-of-pearl shell, is becoming a gourmet rarity. Among the locally caught seafood featuring on menus are lobster, scallops, chancre and spider crabs, clams and shrimps. Mussels and prawns are imported, and oysters, which used to thrive along the shores of the east coast, are now successfully farmed.

*Fisherman's catch
at Bonne Nuit*

65

In the past the basic ingredients of many traditional Jersey dishes were dried red and white beans, formerly grown on every farm on the island. The Jersey Bean Crock, said to be the origin of baked beans, is a variation of the French cassoulet, comprising five different kinds of dried beans, pigs' trotter, belly of pork or shin of beef, carrot and onion. Nowadays the dish is rarely made, but Jersey beans are making a comeback.

The unappetisingly named Jersey 'black butter' is in fact a type of apple preserve. This used to be produced in vast quantities every autumn, a typical recipe comprising 700lb of apples, 10 gallons of cider, 20lb of sugar, 24 lemons and 3lb of spices. Cooking carried on all day and night, with family members stirring the huge pot and making merry with song and dance. The hot sticky mixture was then stored in jars, to last until the following autumn. The centuries-old tradition is kept alive by the Jersey Young Farmers Club who hold black butter nights in November and a few other enthusiasts who make it in smaller quantities. Among other Jersey specialities are conger eel soup, made with the head of the eel boiled in milk and garnished with marigold flower petals, *Des bourdélots*, apples baked in pastry, *des Mèrvelles* or Jersey Wonders, doughnut-like cakes, traditionally cooked as the tide went out, and cabbage loaf – crusty white bread baked in large cabbage leaves, and still sold in some bakeries.

*Traditional produce at Hamptonne
Country Life Museum*

The humble prawn sandwich

Restaurant at Samarès Manor

Cider used to be the drink of the island and large quantities were exported from the mid-17th century to the mid-19th century. One of the few places where it is made today is La Mare Wine Estate, St Mary, which also produces Jersey's only wines along with home-made mustards, jams, jellies and Jersey 'black butter' *(see Route 3, page 36)*.

Restaurants

Jersey has around 200 restaurants, including a handful which might compete with the best in London. The island works hard to promote its food, each May hosting the Menu du Terroir competition when restaurants, pubs and cafés show off the best of the island's produce. Retired tax-exiles and prosperous resident financiers and lawyers ensure a year-round clientèle for the best restaurants and even the discerning French come across the Channel on day trips to indulge their palates.

Cream tea at Jersey Pottery

The gastronomic scene in St Helier is looking up, with the Michelin-starred Bohemia Restaurant *(see page 68)* and the chic new restaurants in the revamped Royal Yacht Hotel. Otherwise the best choice of restaurants is found at Gorey, St Aubin and tiny Rozel in the north.

Most beaches have at least one café, some serving mussels and chips, crab sandwiches, home-made cakes and cream teas. The latter can vary from the pre-packed variety to freshly made scones with lashings of thick Jersey cream and strawberry jam.

The restaurants in this selection are listed according to the following price categories: £££ = expensive (over £65 for two); ££ = moderate (£35–65 for two); £ = Inexpensive (under £35 for two). Price brackets do not include wine.

Gorey

Borsalino Rocque, La Grande Route des Sablons, Grouville, tel: 01534 852111. Known for its seafood. Book in advance for a table in the floral conservatory. Music from 11pm. ££–£££

Castle Green, Gorey (opposite the Castle), tel: 01534 840218. Award-winning gastropub using fish, local produce and offering a menu which changes daily. ££

Jersey Pottery Restaurant, Gorey Village, Grouville, tel: 01534 850850. A favourite among islanders for excellent value seafood and delightful garden setting *(see page 48)*. ££–£££

Suma's, Gorey Hill, Gorey, tel: 01534 853291. Fresh, innovative cuisine in a stylish restaurant overlooking Gorey harbour and castle. English cuisine with Mediterranean and Oriental overtones. Good value set lunches – reserve a table al fresco. ££–£££

The Village Bistro, Gorey Village, Grouville, tel: 01534 853429. Imaginative dishes at affordable prices with emphasis on locally sourced seafood. Excellent value. ££

St Aubin

Boat House, One North Quay, tel: 01534 744226. Stylish restaurant and bar in a glass and timber building on the harbour's edge. £££

La Barca, Bulwarks, St Aubin, tel: 01534 44275. Cheerful Italian trattoria by the harbour. ££

Old Court House Inn, St Aubin, tel: 01534 46433. Historic harbour-side house, converted into a hotel. Specialities are lobster, crayfish and crab. Choice of eating areas includes a conservatory, main restaurant, harbour-view terrace and garden courtyard. £££

Salty Dog Bar and Bistro, Le Boulevard, St. Aubin, tel: 01534 742760. Very popular for new world cuisine and strong on seafood. Contempory music is very much part of the scene. ££–£££

Fresh fish

St Brelade

Hotel l'Horizon, St Brelade's Bay, tel: 01534 743101. The Crystal Room and the Grill offer bay views and some of the best cuisine on the island. The Brasserie within the leisure centre serves light meals. ££ (Brasserie); £££ (Crystal Room, Grill)

Jambo, St Brelade's Bay, tel: 01534 745801 Bay-view restaurant, specialising in Peking and Szechuan dishes. ££

Pizza Express, St Brelade's Bay, tel: 01534 499049. The usual pizzas served in an award-winning glass building with fine views of the bay. £

Wayside Café, St Brelade's Bay. Appealing seaside café serving steaks, salads, seafood, home made cakes and puddings. Lovely views from terrace. No bookings. £

Zanzibar, St Brelade's Bay, tel: 01534 741081. African-style lodge above the beach, offering seafood dishes with an exotic twist. ££–£££

St Clement

Green Island Restaurant, Green Island, St Clement, tel: 01534 857787. Facing Green Island. Excellent value seafood, including scallops, sand eels and sea bass. ££.

St Helier

Old Court House Inn

Bistro Central, 7–11 Don Street, St Helier, tel: 01534 876933. French-style bistro, in the heart of St Helier. Specialities are fish and shell fish. £££.

Bohemia Restaurant, Green Street, St Helier, tel: 01534 880588. The island's finest food served in the stylish modern surroundings of the Club Hotel and Spa. Also serves imaginative and affordable bar snacks. £££ (restaurant); £ (bar)

Café des Artistes, King Street, St Helier, tel: 01534 639990. Café and brasserie within Voisins department store in the centre of St Helier. £

La Capannina, 65–67 Halkett Place, St Helier, tel: 01534 34602. Smart Italian restaurant, popular with businessmen at lunchtime. £££

City Restaurant and Bar, 75–77 Halkett Place, tel: 01534 510096. Contemporary café, with internet facilities (free access with a meal). £–££

Green Olive, 1 Anley Street, St Helier, tel: 01534 728198. Inventive vegetarian fare along with seafood and chicken, using fresh local produce. Leave room for the delicious desserts. ££

The Museum Brasserie, Jersey Museum, Weighbridge, St Helier, tel: 01534 510069. International cuisine. Choose from set menus or simple à la carte menus. Open all day for coffee and cakes. £–££

The Olive Branch, 39 Colomberie, St Helier, tel: 01534 615993. Stylish place for Italian cusine: fresh pasta and excellent pizzas, cooked in wood-burning oven. £–££

St Lawrence

Hamptonne Café, Hamptonne Country Life Museum, La Rue de la Patente, tel: 01534 863955. Home-baked light lunches and snacks. Specializes in Jersey traditional fare such as Bean Crock, Jersey Wonders and cabbage leaves. Must pay museum entrance fee to enter café. £

St Martin

Château La Chaire, Rozel Bay, St Martin, tel: 01534 863354. Part of the Château La Chaire Hotel, offering the best cuisine on the north coast. Good-value set lunches. £££

Le Frère, Rozel Hill, St Martin, tel: 01534 861000. Good value seafood restaurant with superb views across to France from the terrace. ££.

The Hungry Man, Rozel Bay, tel: 01534 863227. Quirky little café renowned for its fabulous crab sandwiches and bacon rolls. £

The Navigator, Harre de Rozel, tel: 01534 861444. Come for king prawns, bouillabaisse or linguini lobster and enjoy the harbour views. For the navigator seafood platter order 24 hours in advance. ££

St Ouen's Bay

Big Vern's, La Grande Route des Mieilles, tel: 01534 481705. Overlooking the pounding waves of St Ouen's and full of hip surfers and happy families. Open all day, from breakfast to sunset suppers. £–££

St Peter

The Carvery, Les Charrières Hotel, St Peter, tel: 01534 481480. Very popular for Sunday roast lunch. Dinner only Monday to Saturday. ££

St Saviour

Longueville Manor, Longueville Road, St Saviour, tel: 01534 25501. Award-winning restaurant serving gourmet cuisine in oak-panelled dining room. Vegetarian and children's menus available. £££

Moulin de Lecq

Pubs

Grève de Lecq

Moulin de Lecq, Grève de Lecq, tel: 01534 482818. 14th-century inn, with a working water mill. Barbecue, fish dishes and snacks. Particularly good for families, as it has a play area. £

Ouaisné Bay

Old Smugglers' Inn, Ouaisné Bay, tel: 01534 741510. Very popular pub, originally 17th-century cottages. Good choice of food from sandwiches and snacks to chicken satay and seafood ragout.

Portelet Bay

Old Portelet Inn, Portelet, St Brelade, tel: 01534 741899. Converted farmhouse in a scenic spot above the bay. Standard pub grub. Indoor and outdoor play area for children. Live entertainment most nights.

St Peter's Village

The Star & Tipsy Toad, St Peter's village, St Peter, tel: 01534 485556. Home-brewed ales such as Tipsy Toad or Horny Toad.

Old Smugglers' Inn

Outdoor Activities

Adventure Sports

Pure Adventure (tel: 01534 769165, www.purejersey.com) organize 25 different sporting activities including blokarting, skydiving, rockclimbing, absailing, coasteering, surfing, sea kayaking and kiteboarding.

Beaches

Cycling options

Jersey provides acres of sandy beaches and numerous rockpools for shrimp and crab fishing. The best beaches for youngsters are St Brelade's and St Aubin's where the sand shelves gently and the waters are normally calm. In contrast, wild and windswept St Ouen's has great waves for surfing or bodyboarding. Beauport east of St Brelade's is one of the loveliest and least crowded bays.

Cycling

See page 57 for cycling on Jersey. For bike hire in St Helier, try Zebra Cycles, 9 Esplanade, tel: 01534 736556 (www.zebrahire.com); in St Aubin call Jersey Cycle Tours, tel: 01534 746780.

Golf

To play at the Royal Jersey Golf Club at Grouville, tel: 01534 854416 (www.royaljersey.com), or La Moye at St Brelade, tel: 01534 743401; both are 18-hole and require a handicap certificate. Anyone can play at Les Mielles, St Ouen's Bay, tel: 01534 482787, Wheatlands, St Peter, tel: 01534 888844, Les Ormes, St Brelade, tel: 01534 499077, and Jersey Recreation Grounds, Grève d'Azette, St Clement, tel: 01534 721938.

Golf at Grouville

Tennis

Courts are available at the Jersey Recreation Grounds at Grève d'Azette, St Clement, tel: 01534 721938, the Quennevais Sports Centre, St Brelade, tel: 01534 490909, and there are indoor courts at Les Ormes, St Brelade, tel: 01534 744464.

Boat trips

Standard cruiser trips along the south coast depart from Albert Quay, St Helier, tel: 01534 732466 (www.jersey cruises.com). More exciting tours, such as visiting offshore reefs and seeing wildlife, can be booked through RIB Voyages, tel: 01534 630857 or 07797 731933 (www. islandribvoyages.com).

Fishing

Wrasse, bass, grey mullet, black bream, pollack, garfish, mackerel and conger eel are all caught offshore. For boat fishing trips from St Helier, contact David Nuth, tel: 01534 858046 or 07797 728316 (www.tarkaseatrips. com). The piers on the north coast are popular for rod fishing. Low tide is the best time for finding prawns, crabs and small fish in the rock pools. In St Aubin during spring tides razor fish can be enticed from the sands by sprinkling salt on their key-shaped holes.

Diving

The Jersey sea is clean, visibility is good and marine life plentiful. The Bouley Bay Diving School is a PADI 5-star diving centre which welcomes divers of all standards, including beginners. Tel: 01534 866990 (www.scubadivingjersey.com).

More experienced divers can visit the wrecks of ships sunk in World War II and other vessels which have been deliberately scuttled to provide shelter for marine life.

Leisure and Fitness

The Waterfront Centre at St Helier, tel: 01534 734524, features a fitness club and Aqua Splash with leisure and outdoor pools, slides, sundeck and diving area.

Sailing

The waters around the Channel Islands are popular for yachting but the sunken reefs, big tides and strong currents make it unsuitable for inexperienced sailors. Boats can be chartered for those with experience, alternatively skippers can be hired. For yacht charter and tuition contact www.jerseysailing.com, tel: 01534 851983.

Surfing at St Ouen's

Surfing and windsurfing

St Ouen's Bay has excellent surf and is the venue for international surfing competitions in summer. Inexperienced surfers should always keep to the areas between flags, which are surveyed by lifeguards. Companies along the bay hiring out surf equipment and offering tuition include the Jersey Surfing School at the Watersplash, tel: 01534 484005, and Atlantic Waves, tel: 01534 744157, www.cisurf.com.

St Aubin's Bay, St Brelade's Bay, Grouville and St Ouen's Bay are the most popular for windsurfing.

Other watersports

Waterskiing, wakeboarding, speed boat, banana rides, canoes and rowing boats are available at St Brelade's Bay, St Aubin (La Haule slipway) and at the Gorey watersports Centre, Grouville. For seakayaking trips contact Kayak Adventures, www.jerseykayakadventures.co.uk.

For further information on sports on the island, go to the tourist office website on www.jersey.com/active.

Workout at Fort Regent

Getting There

Package holidays to Jersey, either by sea or air, can be arranged through British tour operators. Alternatively, most of the hotels, guest houses and self-catering establishments on the island can arrange travel for you, as well as travel insurance and car rental. Flight details are available from any travel agent in the UK or from Jersey specialists such as Channel Island Travel Services (tel: 01534 496600; www.jerseytravel.com) who can take care of flights from UK airports, sea travel or car hire.

By air

Direct flights operate to Jersey from around 25 UK airports and several European airports. The main airlines operating services to Jersey from the UK are Flybe (tel: 0871 5226100, www.flybe.com) which fly from 13 airports, including Gatwick; British Airways (tel: 0870 8509850, www.ba.com) from Gatwick; flybmi (tel: 0870 6070555, www.flybmi.com) from Heathrow; and Thomsonfly (tel: 0870 1900737, www.thomsonfly.com) from four airports, including Luton. Prices vary hugely and it's worth shopping around for low-cost flights. Considerable savings can be made by booking online. Aurigny Air Services (tel: 01481 822886, www.aurigny.com) provide a Channel Island hopping service between Jersey, Alderney and Guernsey.

Taxis are available at Jersey airport and a bus leaves every 20 minutes (30 minutes in winter) for St Helier.

By sea

Condor Ferries (tel: 0870 2435140, www.condorferries.com) operate a high-speed 'Wavepiercer' catamaran service to Jersey. In winter it runs from Weymouth only; from April to October there are regular crossings from Weymouth and Poole. The catamaran, which takes cars as well as passengers, takes around 3 hours if you go to Jersey direct, slightly longer if you go via Guernsey. Bad weather conditions can lead to the cancellation of the crossing. Condor also operate a traditional ferry (Mon–Sat all year) which takes about 10 hours to Jersey from Portsmouth.

Inter-island ferries and France

Condor *(see above)* operate a high-speed car ferry service between St Malo and Jersey (2hrs 30 mins). Manche-Îles-Express (tel: 01534 880756, www.manche-iles-express.com) operate seasonal services between St Helier and Carteret and Granville in Normandy, and between Gorey and Carteret. Passports are required for France.

Condor Ferries operate day trips to Guernsey, with connections on to Sark and Herm.

Luxury at the Atlantic Hotel, St Brelade's Bay

73

Taxis can take you from the airport to St Helier

Vintage bus at St Catherine's Bay

Car hire

Car hire prices in the Channel Islands are among the cheapest in Europe, and the price of fuel is lower than in the UK. The maximum speed limit is 40 mph (64km/h). Visitors wishing to hire a car must produce a valid driving licence and be aged 21 and over; some firms impose an upper age limit. Car hire companies are abundant and competitive.

Hire firms include: Avis, St Peter, tel: 01534 519100, www.avisjersey.co.uk; Europcar, Jersey Airport, freephone 0800 7350735, www.europcarjersey.com; Hertz, Jersey Airport, freephone 0800 7351014, www.hertz-jersey.com; and Aardvark Zebra Hire, 9 Esplanade, St Helier, tel: 01534 736556, www.zebrahire.com.

Buses

Connex Transport Jersey, tel: 01534 877772 (www.mybus.je), provides a network of buses from Liberation Station in St Helier. The Connex Explorer service links over 20 island attractions and beaches during the summer season.

Cycling

See pages 57 and 70.

Driving

The island's maximum speed-limit is 40mph (64km/h), reduced to 30mph or 20mph (48 or 32km/h) in some town areas and to 15mph (24 km/h) on Green Lanes *(see page 52)*. In the event of an accident, call the police on 612612 or, in an emergency, 999.

Parking

In St Helier the easiest option is to park in one of the five multi-storey car parks. Parking cards (or 'scratchcards'), which must be displayed, are available from garages and many shops, but, apart from Sand Street, *not* in the car parks themselves. The cards are also used in a few other busy areas, but parking elsewhere is usually free. Some free parking, however, is controlled by parking discs, provided by car-hire companies or obtainable from St Helier Town Hall.

Le Petit Train

Small trains with guided commentaries operate from St Helier. One does a half-hour tour of the town, departing from Liberation Square, and the two others skirt the bay to St Aubin, starting opposite the Grand Hotel. Evening trips operate in summer. For bookings, tel: 07797 777199.

St Helier's esplanade train

Facts for the Visitor

Travel documents

No passport is required for visitors travelling from the British Isles and the Republic of Ireland but airlines now require photographic ID in order to travel.

Tourist information

Jersey Tourism, in Liberation Place, St Helier, has a wealth of information on the island and can also arrange accommodation. It is open June–Sept, Mon–Sat 8.30am–5.30pm, Sun 8.30am–2.15pm, and off-season, Mon–Fri 9am–5pm, Sat 9am–1pm, tel: 01534 448800. Most of the information can be accessed on its website, www.jersey.com.

Sightseeing

Most attractions are free for young children and substantial reductions are given to senior citizens and students.

Banks

Although Jersey has its own currency, in the same denominations as UK notes and coins, British money is freely accepted on the island, as are most UK credit and debit cards. A few shops accept euros.

Post offices

The main post office is located in Broad Street, St Helier and is open Mon–Fri 8.30am–5pm, Sat 9am–2pm. Jersey postage stamps, available from post offices and some shops, must be used on all mail.

Telephone and internet

Public call boxes take coins or credit cards. The area code for Jersey from the UK is 01534, STD codes for the UK from Jersey are the same as those used from the UK. Some 'Pay as you Go' phones do not function in Jersey and certain mobile networks require a roaming facility. Calls received or made in Jersey with UK mobiles are usually charged as international. Internet access is available at Jersey Library, Halkett Place, St Helier, tel: 01534 759991, and at City Restaurant and Bar *(see page 68)*.

Time

The Channel Islands follow Greenwich Mean Time (GMT).

Opening times

Bank, shop and post office opening times are generally the same as in the UK. Most of the museums and tourist attractions are open Apr–Oct, daily 9am or 10am–5pm.

Young children usually go free

Relaxing after a shopping trip

Downtown St Helier

Public holidays

These are the same as those of the UK with the addition of Liberation Day on 9 May.

Shopping

The chief attraction of shopping in Jersey is the duty and VAT-free goods. However, this is not apparent in many shops which put up prices for 'shipping costs'. The main centre is St Helier, with its pedestrianised shopping streets and food and fish market. The shops are similar to those you would find on a UK high street, but with an abundance of cosmetics. Several craft centres are dotted around the island, Jersey Pottery *(see page 48)* being the most famous.

Nightlife

Nightlife is mainly confined to St Helier and consists of pubs and discos primarily aimed at young residents and tourists. The *Jersey Evening Post* is the best place to find out about performances by live bands, jazz concerts, DJs, etc. A new focus of nightlife is the Waterfront Centre in St Helier, whose attractions include the Liquid and Envy Nightclub, Chicago Rock Café and the 10-screen Cineworld (tel: 0871 2002000). Pubs are open on weekdays 9am–11pm, Sun 11am–11pm. For theatre, music and the arts, *see page 63*.

Health and medical services

Visitors requiring medical attention should call: 01534 616883 Mon–Fri 8.30am–4.30pm to be connected to a GP surgery who will issue an appointment and the location of the surgery for that day. There is no charge for visitors from the UK and other countries with a reciprocal agreement. Out of hours, call the General Hospital in St Helier which has a 24 hour emergency unit, tel: 01534 622000.

Emergencies

In an emergency, dial 999 for police, fire, ambulance or sea rescue.

Disabled access

Details of attractions, accommodation and parking for the disabled are available from Jersey Tourism *(see Tourist information page 75)*. Special parking areas are available for Blue Badge holders. Public conveniences for the disabled, fitted with radar locks, can be found in all the main centres and at most beaches. A shopmobility scheme operates from St Helier's Sand Street car park. Electric scooters, chairs and manual pushchairs are available Mon-Sat 10am–4.30pm; prior booking advisable (tel 01534 739672 or 07797 73697, www.shopmobility.org.je).

Jersey for Children

With its sandy beaches, clean seas and rock pools, Jersey is ideal for children. Most of the museums and attractions on the island are geared to all ages, particularly the **Durrell Wildlife Conservation Trust** *(see page 50)*, **Maritime Museum** *(see page 15)*, **Living Legend** *(see page 23)* and **Hamptonne Country Life Museum** *(see page 35)*. Another favourite is **Elizabeth Castle** *(see page 20)*, especially the journey across to the islet in the amphibious ferry.

The **Amaizin Maze and Adventure Park** (La Hougue Farm, La Grande Route de St Pierre, St Peter, tel: 01534 482116, www.jerseymaze.com) combine a maze constructed entirely of the cereal crop maize with an Adventure Park featuring toboggan run, go-karts, tractor rides, water pistol range and lots more.

Taking aim at the water pistol range

Art and craft enthusiasts will enjoy **Glaze Craze** at Jersey Pottery *(see page 48)*, where you can paint and decorate a plain mug, plate or pig and have it glazed by the pottery.

Beach pursuits

At **Treasures of the Earth** (summer, daily 9.30am–5pm), on La Route de l'Etacq, St Ouen, a journey through caverns, grottos and 'The Magic Temple' reveals glowing crystallised minerals, gemstones, fossils and prehistoric creatures.

Young children will be quite content to spend the day messing around in rock pools, fishing for shrimps, crabs and devil fish. Every beach shop sells cheap nets and buckets. The best beaches for kids are St Brelade's and St Aubin's. However, older children who are good swimmers will love body surfing on the waves at St Ouen's. Boogy boards are available for hire at various points.

The island has several parks and gardens, many with play areas for children. **Coronation Park** at Millbrook is one of the most popular for children. **Sunset Flower Centre**, behind St Ouen's Bay, has an indoor exhibition of fantasy-themed sand sculptures and a pond stocked with koy carp which feed on pellets sold on the premises.

Fort Regent in St Helier (tel: 01534 500200) provides a range of sport and leisure facilities including bowling, table tennis, short tennis, badminton, snooker and a children's play area. For swimming, head to **Aqua Splash** on the waterfront (tel: 01534 734524), which has a leisure pool with wave machine, bubble pool and spa, outdoor pool with flumes, tyre ride and sun terrace.

Jersey Bowl on the airport road, St Peter (tel: 01534 490444), is an 18-lane centre with a Quaser area, games room and indoor and outdoor play areas for children.

For a tour of St Helier or trip to the harbour village of St Aubin, take **Le Petit Train** *(see page 74)*.

A new friend

St Helier's Radisson SAS Hotel

La Bonne Vie

Get a good night's sleep at the Grand

Accommodation

Jersey has 130 registered hotels and guest houses, and 24 self-catering premises. Bookings can be made through Jersey Tourism. For a copy of the accommodation brochure call: 01534 448050 or download a copy from their website, www.jersey.com.

Hotel selection

The selection below is listed according to the following categories: **££££** (over £190 per night double); **£££** (£140–190); **££** (£85–140); **£** (under £85).

St Helier

La Bonne Vie, Roseville St, tel: 01534 735955; www.labonnevie-guesthouse-jersey.com. This is a charming Victorian guest house close to a beach and pool. **£**

The Club Hotel and Spa, Green Street, tel: 01534 876500; www.theclubjersey.com. Chic boutique hotel with a Michelin-starred restaurant, spa club, outdoor pool. **££££**

Grand Jersey, Esplanade, tel: 01534 722301; www.grandjersey.com. A multi-million pound revamp has brought high-tech luxury to the Grand, with swish furnishings, pools, fitness suite, etc. **£££–££££**

Hotel de France, St Saviour's Road, tel: 01534 614000; www.defrance.co.uk. Elegant and comfortable with a new pool/spa complex. **£££**

Millbrook House, Rue de Trachy, Millbrook, tel: 01534 733036; www.millbrookhousehotel.com. Delightful country house hotel set in large peaceful park and gardens. **££**

Royal Yacht, Weighbridge, tel: 01534 720511; www.theroyalyacht.com. This 1930s hotel has undergone a £25 million extension, with luxury spa, indoor pool, champagne bar and chic eateries. **££££**

SAS Radisson, Rue de l'Etau, tel: 01534 769744; www.sasradisson.com. Controversial new block on the waterfront; its 195 rooms are geared towards business travellers rather than tourists. £££–££££

Uplands, St John's Road, Mont à l'Abbé, tel: 01534 873006; www.morvanhotels.com. A family-run hotel, based around a set of old granite buildings and located in its own farmland. ££

Bouley Bay

Water's Edge Hotel, Bouley Bay, Trinity, tel: 01534 862777; www.watersedgehotel.co.je. Above pebble beach, with beautiful views. ££

Gorey

Moorings Hotel, **Gorey Pier**, tel: 01534 853633; www.themooringshotel.com. Smart little hotel at the foot of Mont Orgueil, noted for its cuisine. 16 rooms only. ££

Rozel

Chateau La Chaire, Rozel Bay, St Martin, tel: 01534 863354; www.chateau-la-chaire.co.uk. Smart, country house hotel, at the foot of Rozel Valley. Well known for its cuisine *(see page 68)*. ££££

Old Court House Inn

St Aubin

Harbour View, St Aubin Harbour, tel: 01534 741585; www.harbourviewjersey.com. Charming guest house with garden bistro. 13 rooms. £

Old Court House Inn, St Aubin Harbour, tel: 01534 746433; www.oldcourthousejersey.com. Fine harbourview 15th-century building. *See page 67* for restaurant. ££–£££

St Brelade's Bay

Atlantic Hotel, Le Mont de la Pulente, St Brelade, tel: 01534 744101; www.slh.com. Magnificent views over St Ouen's Bay. Michelin-starred restaurant, health and leisure centre, indoor and outdoor pools, tennis courts. ££££

Golden Sands, St Brelade's Bay, tel: 01534 741241. Modern hotel, well-situated with steps down to the beach. ££

L'Horizon, St Brelade's Bay, tel: 01534 743101; www.handpicked.co.uk/lhorizon. Luxurious and civilised, with cool contemporary decor; overlooking bay. ££££

St Brelade's Bay Hotel, St Brelade's Bay, tel: 01534 746141; www.stbreladesbayhotel.com. Elegant hotel in large gardens, with the beach just across the road. £££–££££

St Saviour

Longueville Manor, St Saviour, tel: 01534 725501; www.longuevillemanor.com. Country-house hotel in large grounds, renowned for its cuisine *(see page 69)*. ££££

St Brelade's Bay Hotel

Index

Register with
HotelClub.com
and get £10!

At *HotelClub.com*, we reward our Members with discounts and free stays in their favourite hotels. As a Member, every booking made by you through *HotelClub.com* will earn you Member Dollars.

When you register, we will credit your account with *£10* which you can use for your next booking! The equivalent of *£10* will be credited in US$ to your Member account (as *HotelClub Member Dollars*). All you need to do is log on to *www.HotelClub.com/compactguides*. Complete your details, including the Membership Number and Password located on the back of the *HotelClub.com* card.

Over 3.5 million Members already use Member Dollars to pay for all or part of their hotel bookings. Join now and start spending Member Dollars whenever and wherever you want – you are not restricted to specific hotels or dates!

With great savings of up to 60% on over 25,000 hotels across 120 countries, you are sure to find the perfect location for business or pleasure.
Happy travels from *HotelClub.com!*